Indoor Gardening

Learn to Grow a Garden in Your Home From Setup to Harvest

(How You Can Grow Vegetables Herbs Flowers and Fruits Along With Tips for Beginners)

Stephen Dudley

Published By **Phil Dawson**

Stephen Dudley

Indoor Gardening: Learn to Grow a Garden in Your Home From Setup to Harvest (How You Can Grow Vegetables Herbs Flowers and Fruits Along With Tips for Beginners)

ISBN   978-1-998901-11-1

Legal & Disclaimer

The information contained in this ebook is not designed to replace or take the place of any form of medicine or professional medical advice. The information in this ebook has been provided for educational & entertainment purposes only.

The information contained in this book has been compiled from sources deemed reliable, and it is accurate to the best of the Author's knowledge; however, the Author cannot guarantee its accuracy and validity and cannot be held liable for any errors or omissions. Changes are periodically made to this book. You must consult your doctor or get professional medical advice before using any of the suggested remedies, techniques, or information in this book.

Table Of Contents

Chapter 1: Why Should I Have A Garden Inside?

House Plants and Their Benefits

It can be hard to maintain good health and eat healthy foods in today's fast-paced world. Globally, people are more mindful of their health. People try to eat healthier foods, exercise more and live a happier and healthier lifestyle.

An indoor garden can provide many benefits to your health, and enhance your quality of life. After you are fully aware of all the benefits, you will want house plants on your next shopping list.

Many people know that having your own backyard garden is beneficial, but not everyone has enough space. An obvious solution is to grow your own garden indoors. Houseplants are beautiful and can create a lovely atmosphere in your home. It will supply you and your family lots of fresh nutrients, and improve the quality of the air inside your home.

Plants have a profound influence on any environment. They can bring nature inside your home, and act as natural air fresheners. Fresh fruits and vegetables will be ready to go on your table, and you can stock up on fresh produce for your refrigerator. Here are some benefits to houseplants.

Oxygen

We all know plants produce oxygen. The fresher the room, the more plants there are. A peaceful environment is guaranteed to be enhanced by plants. I am curious if you are aware of the fact that plants are capable of helping to prevent colds, reduce stress levels, stop headaches, and to remove contaminants.

Colds

It has been proven that indoor plants can reduce cold related illnesses by as much as 30 percent. This can be explained with a lower dust load and an increase humidity.

Contaminants

Because we all breathe the same air continuously, even in winter, harmful substances can be inhaled through our doors and windows. Indoor plants can prevent this from happening by removing VOC's or volatile organic compounds (VOCs) that can cause nausea, headaches, as well as other illnesses.

Headaches

The most common cause of headaches is stale, stuffy indoor air. By filling your house with plants, this can help to reduce or eliminate the symptoms. Because plants absorb carbon dioxide in the air and release oxygen into it, this condition can be eliminated. This will make your home less likely be stale.

Happiness

You will feel a sense of well-being and happiness when you bring nature into your house in the form of houseplants. Plants have a relaxing effect on people, and they make them feel more optimistic. Numerous studies have found that patients who face a window looking out onto the garden or from their hospital bed recover faster than those who sit facing inwards.

Mental Health

It is possible to lift your mood by caring for a pet, or plants, if you feel lonely or depressed. It will give your mind a purpose, provide motivation to get out of bed each morning, and aid in improving your mental health.

Blood Pressure

The calming effects that plants can have on your immediate environment are of many benefits. It decreases stress, and it has been proven that people with indoor plants tend to have lower blood pressure.

Carbon Dioxide

The photosynthesis process is where carbon dioxide is removed from the atmosphere by plants. This helps to make the air purer and reduces drowsiness in the residents.

Treatments

Many indoor plants are capable of reducing pain.

Allergies

Children who are exposed to plants early in their lives are less likely to become allergic later on. They will develop tolerance and become intolerant to these allergens. This is similar in nature to an allergy shot.

Cigarette Smoke

You may find yourself living with someone who smokes. Indoor plants can prove to be a huge help for those who smoke. They can remove harmful chemicals found in cigarette smoke from the air and help to clean it. You can make it even more effective by including a Peace Lily or two with your indoor plants.

A Healthy Brain

Why would you not feel more hopeful and inspired by plants that have beautiful flowers? It will boost your mood and help you think more clearly.

Clean Air

Photosynthesis lets plants release oxygen in the air they are in. They filter chemicals to improve the quality and air quality. The result? Your home's air will be cleaner if there are plants around.

Congestion

Eucalyptus is one of the plants that has been shown to reduce congestion and phlegm. The same substance can be found as a remedy for this condition.

Humidifiers

It is better to invest in indoor plants than a humidifier, especially if you live near very dry areas. The natural humidity is increased by plants, which soften the air.

Sleep

Plants can improve your sleep quality. One of the plants that emit oxygen at night is the Gerbera Daisy. This beautiful flower will give you a great night's sleep.

Morale

Offices will often have many potted plant collections. This is because indoor plants have been a benefit to companies for many years. They know that indoor plants are more productive than their employees and can improve employee morale.

Indoor Plants and their Advantages

While indoor plants offer many benefits, there are also challenges. We should now highlight some of those challenges that you may face when growing plants indoors.

Houseplants will bring the beauty and serenity of nature into your living space. They purify the air by removing pollutants like formaldehyde (trichloroethylene) and benzene. There are some downsides to these plants, mostly because of the way they are chosen and maintained.

More Work

Plants that live in containers require more water than plants that grow in the soil. This is because containers dry faster than soil. Gardenias, for instance, that grow outdoors need only water two times per week. Indoor plants require watering more often. Indoor plants should be regularly fed and must be kept clean. As they will tend to grow towards sunlight, they may bend to one end and need to be turned frequently.

Humidity and Water Needs

Indoor plants require approximately fifty percent humidity to thrive. It is possible for indoor plants to suffer from dry winter months because of the drying effect of heating. This is not a big problem. You can put humidifiers around the plants. If you prefer, place your plants in a tray containing water and pebbles.

Mold and Fungus

Indoor plants may not have enough light and moisture. This may cause them to develop molds. Also, moldy or bacterial infections on the leaves may cause permanent damage and even death. Mold spores, along with other pollutants, can be released into the air and infect you.

These infections can often be treated easily. If your plant is covered in whiteflies, wash it under the hot water. Your plants may have brown spots, which is a sign that they are getting too much moisture. You can water them less often.

Vacation Care

Your indoor plants should be fine if you're going away for a weekend. You may need to look for another solution if a neighbor or friend can't take care of your plants.

Consider these options: Use plastic sheets to create enough moisture to sustain your plants. Or, set up a system with buckets of water and pieces made from natural fiber to water the plants. You might also choose to buy a watering method that operates according to a specific timer.

Chapter 2: Best Herbs

A windowill filled with fresh herbs can be the best gift that a city dweller can offer. It takes only a little bit of sunshine to make fresh herbs. And it will take a few weeks for you to use them in your home. Don't be discouraged if you are just starting to grow plants. You might have some difficulties along the way but if your perseverance and start slowly, you will soon experience the great satisfaction of adding home-grown basil or fresh lemongrass in your next dish. This chapter will explain how to choose the right plants for your indoor herb gardens. This guideline is intended for both those with green thumbs and beginners.

The Easy Choices

Bay Tree

Laurus Nobilis is the best variety of Laurus for cooking. It is slow growing. It can become scale-prone if it gets too dry. To remove scale, wash the leaves using dishwashing detergent. Rinse the leaves well.

Chives

This herb is easy to cultivate because it requires less sunlight. Grolau is the best choice for an indoor garden, as it was specially bred.

Kaffir Lime Tree

Thai cuisine often uses the leaves of this tree. The plant will develop its full potential quickly if you provide citrus food.

Lemongrass

This herb can be grown without soil, which is quite amazing. Next time you are at your local market buy a stalk without the bottom. After trimming its top, place it in a container. Make sure to add enough water to moisten the stem. Within a short time, the stalk will produce roots as well new sprouts. A lot of stalks will sprout, which you can easily remove and use for your meals.

Mint

Mint is a invasive plant. It can overtake any area. Choose peppermint if mint tea is your preference. It's best to have a small amount. Because spearmint is used in many recipes, you will need a bigger pot.

Parsley

Parsley requires patience. It takes time to grow and needs patience. It requires much less sunlight so it is still well worth the effort.

Vietnamese Coriander

This herb tastes similar in flavor to cilantro, but is easy to grow as it's very reliable and doesn't require any special care. It is one among the easiest herbs you can grow indoors.

More difficult herbs

Oregano

This herb needs plenty of light to thrive so place it in the right place. The Greek variety is an excellent choice for indoor gardens.

Rosemary

Rosemary is a plant that needs lots of sunlight. Place it in a sunny spot. You may need additional light. It doesn't require much moisture so avoid overwatering. Blue Spire Blue Blue and Tuscan Blue are both excellent varieties. Rosemary is a simple herb to grow, and you only need to add a few drops to give your dishes a unique flavor.

Thyme

If you want to grow thyme you will need to be able provide enough light. As it is not widely available in markets, lemon thyme is a good alternative.

The Most Hard Herbs To Grow

Basil

Basil is something we all love. However, it's one of most difficult herbs to cultivate. If you are determined to grow basil, do it during summer when there is optimal sunlight and bright warm days. Spicy Globe and African Blue are great choices. They're also easy to grow indoors. The Thai basil should perform well inside, while the second is an indoor variety.

Cilantro

We call coriander leaves and stems cilantro. It tends to grow flowers and seed instead of the leaves used in food, making it difficult to grow. One way to get the coriander seedlings into your garden is to plant them in plastic trays. Once they are established, you can enjoy them as sprouts. The seeds should be sown thickly. Once the seeds reach 4 inches in height, pull them apart, wash and then enjoy. To save money, you can order coriander plants in bulk from your local pharmacy.

Sage

Avoid overwatering your sage plant. They are extremely sensitive to excess moisture. They can also become mildewed quickly. Dwarf sage, which is compacter and better than regular, is your best bet.

Growing Your Indoors Herb Garden

Fresh pesto and pasta sauce is something you will love if it's also your favorite dish. If so, then there are no other options. Instead of buying pre-grown herbs like basil and cilantro throughout the year. All you need is at most five hours of sunlight daily. All herbs, including basil, mint, bayle, rosemary and savory can be successfully grown indoors. This chapter contains all the information you will need to grow fresh herbs at your home.

The right amount of light

Eighteen-hour vegetative light cycles are common for herb plants. This includes at the very least eight hours of direct sunlight. The more light you provide, the higher the yield. Some herbs require longer hours of sunlight than others. Basil and coriander for example will not flourish without getting at least eight hour of light.

All day long, shine bright light.

Here are some possible solutions.

* The winter months can be dark and the light levels will drop. This is when you need to step in to give your indoor plants an extra boost. Put a bright fluorescent bulb above the plants, and make sure it is on for the appropriate amount of time. This will increase the plants' growth and, in turn, their yield. This will ensure that you have enough basil to make your pesto fresh whenever you want it.

* You could also consider a halide or tungsten light. This small, metal light will give you more light over a greater area. You can also grow herbs to add flavor to all your meals.

Choose the Right Soil

This may sound strange, but some herbs will grow better in poorer soil. It is possible for herbs to develop stronger tastes. Let me elaborate: If herbs grow too quickly, they may produce plain stems. These flavorsome essential oils take a longer time to develop, and if your soil is too rich, they develop too quickly. Slow down when fertilizing.

The Right Soil for Containers

However, this does not mean you can grow your herbs in a container and expect them to flourish. Every plant needs food to grow. It is vital to find the right balance in your plant's food. Here are some tips that will help to explain the growth habits and treatment of different herbs.

* It is vital to regulate the plant's initial growth rate. You need to ensure that the soil mixture contains the correct amount and quality nutrients. Two parts coconut fiber, or coir, to one part perlite. Add twenty percent vermicompost to make worm castings. For every litre soil mix, you can add 1g of hydrated lime. Vermiculite can be used instead.

* Plants also need hormones. For every gallon of soil, add 1 tablespoon kelp meals. This will give the soil microorganisms sufficient food to feed your plants.

The Correct Moisture

Always check the soil surface of your plants. If it feels dry to your touch, it's likely that your plant requires water. You can also simply pick up the container. It should feel too light to touch. You should make holes in all containers. Herbs love soil that is quick draining. After that, you can add small pieces of perlite, broken slate, flat stones, gravel and gravel to your soil. Your herbs will thrive if you water them well but not too often. Let the pot sit until water runs out of the bottom. Never over-water.

Basil will not tolerate water on its stems. Make sure you water around the stem.

After 10 Days, Feeding Time

Allow your herb plants to rest in their pots or containers for approximately ten days before feeding them. Containers can only hold as much soil as the roots will need to absorb it all. This is true even if you have not given your plants any other food. You can use Maxsea 16-16-16 every two weeks.

Additional Boost

Here is an additional tip to help keep your herb plant plants happy. To the water you provide your plants, make sure to add liquid seaweed. The B1 has vitamins and roots hormones. Seaweed acts as a trace nutrients and plant hormone. This additional boost will allow for the production and preservation of essential oils, which give herbs their delicious flavor.

Use herbs only when they are available

Your herb plants should have reached maturity in four to six months and produce enough leaves that you are able harvest them. It is important to carefully remove any leaves that may be damaged or prevent the plant from growing. Some herbs like basil should be harvested before the flowers open. The leaves will begin to show their highest levels of essential oils at the end, which is if the leaves were not left in darkness.

Chapter 3: Growing Indoor Herbs

Specific Tips

Light

This is probably the most important requirement for success when you want to grow herbs, or other plants indoors. Most people neglect to provide adequate lighting to their plants. The ideal hours for daily light are between six and eight. Place your plants into a room with a south-western facing window.

Other options are available if your location is not suitable for plants. Use compact fluorescent lamps in reflector light fixtures. Place them within 4 - 6 inches of your plants. You can also find light fixtures that can be mounted beneath your kitchen cabinet, so that your herbs can be placed on a counter. Make sure to provide adequate lighting for your plants.

If leaves develop brown spots, this could indicate that they are being exposed to too bright light. However, it is uncommon for this to happen. The signs that your plants aren't receiving enough light include long stems with fewer foliage. Because they are not getting enough sunlight, they may be stretching toward the light source. This means that you must provide additional light, or move your plants into an area that receives enough natural light.

Water

Overwatering is the number one mistake people make when trying to grow an indoor herb plant. The plants are not fond of excess moisture.

So how can you tell when to give your herbs water. Keep an eye on your plants. They will tell you by their own means when they feel thirsty. You'll quickly be able to identify the signs they send you. You should allow them to dry properly. This may take from three to five days to more than one week. To determine the moisture level around the root systems, push your finger in the soil to your knuckle. You can take note of every type of herb and count the days between when it will need more water. Once you have that information, follow a consistent watering schedule. They don't like to be given too much water, but they love consistent watering.

What is the best way water your plants? Place your plants in a basin. Be sure to water the plants around the stems, and not the leaves. Allow the water vapor to penetrate the leaves and let them soak for another time. You can then place them back onto the saucers once they have dried completely. It is best to water before work, then let them drain throughout the day. After work, you can place them back on your saucers. Plant roots will rot quickly if there is stagnant water around their saucers.

Yellow leaves are often an indicator of excessive moisture, not underwatering. Too much moisture could cause damage to the roots and lead to the plant's inability to absorb moisture. Leaves will begin to wilt. Many people make the error of giving plants more water after it has dried out. You should first check the soil. Then, look at the bottom of the pot.

Pots & Containers

A pot must have adequate drainage holes.

Terra cotta is the best option for your containers as it allows you to breathe. Any material that protects your window sill or counter can be used to make the saucer. You do not need to put rocks in your pot before you add soil.

Size is the next thing to consider. The larger the pot, better it is for your plants. Pots should be at least six inches wide if you plan to plant individual herbs. Your pot size will increase if multiple herbs are grown in one container. The container to house two or more herbs should have a maximum diameter of ten inches. It should also be approximately eight inches deep.

Soil

The potting earth you use for your pots should be organic and top-quality. It should allow drainage and should never be compacted. A loamy, rich mixture is best. Add one-part perlite for every twenty to five parts soil. Never use soil that you have grown in your garden. It can work outdoors, but won't work indoors.

How do I know if my soil is dry? After watering, the soil should be grainy and not start to form a mass. To test this, squeeze some soil into a small container.

The soil should fall apart when it is released.

I would recommend adding eggshells and other organic matter to the soil of any Mediterranean herbs, including thyme or basil. You can make them flourish with some lime. This is done by placing the eggshells in a food processor along with a small amount of water. Add a tablespoon of this mixture each container or pot that you have prepared for potting soil.

Feeding

The majority of herbs are fairly healthy but will still require good quality organic fertiliser. You can either use liquid seaweed or, if you're able to stand the smell, some fish emulsion. Make sure you plant your herbs for their foliage and not for their flowers. A fertilizer that is low in phosphorous will not promote flowering. You can also use a 1-gallon glass juice jug filled with water. Next, add a tablespoon fish emulsion and make a weak natural fertilizer. You can then water your herb crops with this water solution. Do some research and you may even be able make your fish emulsion at home.

Keep an eye on your plants and ask them for advice when they need more food. If they look like they are not growing properly, then you should feed them. If they have yellowed leaves, it could also indicate that they need feeding. However, you must make sure that the water is not too much.

General Tips

Baby Plants

It is very difficult to grow herbs directly from seeds. This is why it is so much better to purchase baby plants. Consider choosing plants that can be grown indoors. Because plants have difficulty adapting to new environments, it can be difficult for them to move an outdoor plant into their home. Look at local nurseries to make sure you are buying plants that are suitable for your specific climate.

Rotation

You should never leave your plants exactly in the same place. All plants are inclined to grow towards light so rotate all pots weekly.

Cutting

Why are you growing herbs in the first place? They are meant to be eaten. The more you chop leaves, the better your plant will grow. It is important to keep two-thirds the plant intact.

Air

Fresh air is important for your herbs just like humans. A stagnant atmosphere will result in the growth of fungus which can be detrimental to the health of your herbs. To promote proper air circulation, place your containers on a tray that has pebbles. This will allow air to flow through the drain holes at the bottom.

Rest

Many plants enter a state of rest during the winter months, when there is less light. This is normal. Allow them the freedom to do what is best for them and don't overwater. They will soon be growing once the warmer months arrive.

Pests

Make sure to check your plants for pests regularly. Scale appears in the form of rusty brown marks and can be easily treated by washing it with mild soap. If you don't have a mild soap, rub each spot with some rubbing alcohol. Rinse with clean water. Put the aphids in the sink and rinse them off.

Roots

For perennials, you should inspect them at the very least once every twelve month. Examine whether the roots are beginning to grow out of the soil. If the root system is causing problems, it is best to remove the entire plant. The roots should not become brown or form a circle of growth. Healthy roots are white. One of the following options can be used to remove unhealthy roots from your herb plants: After trimming the roots, you can transfer the plant to a larger container. If you don't want your herb garden to grow larger than it already is, remove about an inch from its root bottoms. You can also trim the same amount of soil vertically around the roots to make it smaller. With some additional soil, repot your herb garden. It is important to trim the same amount from the stems as the leaves.

Problems

Don't let your discouragement get you down if you run into problems with an indoor herb garden. There are many qualified people available to provide advice. Begin by calling your local nursery.

How to Grow Indoor Herbs

It is hard to find anything better than growing your own herbs. Growing your herbs yourself allows you to be in complete control of the herbs you use in your food. It allows you to keep a steady supply of the herbs you prefer. It is convenient, but also affordable.

When you learn how to do it correctly, you'll be able start your indoor garden of herbs in no time. We will discuss some of these essentials before you begin.

A Strong Start

You should take your time selecting the right herb plants from the nursery. Look closely at the stems and leaves to make sure there are no blemishes. This could indicate a less-healthy plant. It sounds obvious, but trust me when I say that so many people who first garden are disappointed with the choice they made. These are the questions to ask:

Do you notice any rusty brown spots?

Does the plant seem wilted in any area?

Is this plant in its last days?

Not all plants are suitable for indoor gardening. Start with herbs such as parsley, basil, thyme or sage that can live indoors.

Choose the Right Location

It takes six hours for herbs to get enough sunlight. You must choose the best location for your herbs. They require adequate lighting. Artificial lighting is great if you don't have any sunny areas. HID and LED lights will be the best choices. For artificial light to be effective, plants need between fourteen and sixteen hours of sunlight per day.

You can ensure that your herb plants get enough sunlight, artificial or not.

Another thing to consider is the climate of the area where your herbs will be grown. Not all herbs can withstand cold weather. Keep your non-perennials - plants that only survive one year - from being exposed to cold, particularly during winter months.

Be aware of the climate conditions in your particular area. All these climate elements can have an effect on the growth and health of your plants.

The Correct Container

Some herbs are happy to live in their individual pots. However, others will invade your entire container and drive away all their flat mates. Mint is an invader, so it should always have its own pot. Thyme, though, is a more delicate herb and requires extra care. It is important to do your research before adding different herbs to the same container.

Drainage

Here's a simple rule to help you water your plants. If your soil feels dry it is time to water them. Sometimes, we make mistakes. You should not have a problem as long as your pots allow for adequate drainage.

Because plants take longer to absorb moisture in colder weather, they can rot faster if they are kept wet. Proper drainage is crucial. Always make sure that pots and containers have enough holes in their bottoms. A good drainage is also possible by adding peat and perlite into your potting soil.

Watch out for the Enemy

Many herbs can be grown so that they are bug-free. Particularly if you hate bugs!

It is very easy to avoid insect infestations. Keep your plants healthy by giving them enough moisture. We do not live in perfect world. While some herbs act as repellents for insects, it is possible to still have small, persistent creatures in your indoor gardening.

Be sure to research which bugs are more likely than others to attack which plants. For example, Japanese beetles love basil. Myrtle is a favorite food while rosemary and rosemary are ideal for scales. You should be careful about snails and other pests if your basil and sorrel plants are grown.

If you spot an infestation, it is important to remove all infected leaf immediately. You have many natural options that you can use to get rid of these unwanted guests.

You should remember that not all bugs are a thread for your herb plant plants. Some bugs, such as the lovely ladybugs, should be welcomed to your garden.

Some beneficial insects can help your indoor garden.

How to Harvest

As your partner maintains his beard trimmed, so must you trim your herb plant. Your plants will be less likely to become infected by pests if they have less leaves. Prune the plants every once in a while, but do not remove the big, luscious leaves near the base. These are your plants' solar panels, and they will receive the greatest light.

Take care to balance your trimmings and choosing leaves for your dinner. Use both older leaves and some of the younger ones. When you do this properly, it will stimulate growth. You'll end up with dense, lush plants full of fragrant leaves that you can pick.

Another option

These tips will get you started as an indoor gardener. However, if this is not something you can do, you have other options.

The Urban Cultivator is an automated kitchen garden. The Urban Cultivator uses hydroponics rather than soil-filled pots. All the controls are automated to control the temperature, lighting, and other parameters. This unit will allow you to grow up 40 varieties of micro greens.

Chapter 4: How To Harvest, Dry And Store Herbs

What a delight it will bring you to grow the herbs of choice to harvest whenever you need them. An herb garden can help you enjoy the fresh herbs that aren't available in your local supermarket. Fresh herbs are amazing in taste and aroma. However, to ensure that they are always available throughout the year, preservation is possible. There are many ways to preserve herbs. However, the methods will differ depending upon the type of herbs.

Harvesting Herbs

When the essential oils of your herbs are at their peak, this is the best season to harvest them. It is this oil that gives the plants their distinctive scent. The best time to harvest depends on what part of the plants you intend to harvest, and the use you intend to make of it. Harvesting is possible once your plant has established enough leaves to allow for its continued growth. Even if you remove seventy-five per cent of the foliage, annual herbs will recover. Keep your perennials under control. Never cut more than a tenth of their growth at one time. You should always use pruning shears or a very sharp knife to protect the plant. Each cut should be straight.

It is best to harvest your herbs early in the morning, before the temperature gets too high. Don't harvest the plants before they start to flower. If this happens, your plant's production will drop. If the flowers appear, you should remove them immediately to ensure that your plant continues producing new leaves.

Never spray herbicides on plants you are growing for harvesting. It can be harmful to you. There are many options for pest control and insect management.

Drying Herbs

Low Heat or Air

Traditional herbs are dried either by low heat or with air. Dry herbs are more concentrated and will retain their essence for longer. This should be considered when you use dried herbs in cooking. You'll likely use about a quarter of the fresh herb leaf leaves. Be sure to check the ingredients list before you use them.

Take care to wash the dried herbs in running water. Use paper towels to dry the herbs completely. You can inspect for damaged or dead material, and then remove it. Now tie your herbs together. Tying them too tight will cause the herbs to lose enough air circulation. Place the individual bunches of herbs in a bag made from paper. Keep their stems open and their leaves first. The bags should all have holes punched in the top for ventilation. Now, your herbs can be dried without being contaminated by dust or dirt. Hang your herb bags upright in a dry, warm location that is well ventilated. You can use sheds as well as barns, garages or attics. It will take around a whole month before your herbs dry completely.

Drying Tray

A drying tray is another option. It's especially helpful for herbs that have short stems and for dry leaves. With screen wire attached to a frame, you can create your own trays. Place the herbs in single layer on the trays. Then let them dry in a dry place that is well ventilated. You might need turn the leaves to ensure they dry evenly.

Use heat

Another easy way to dry herbs out is by using heat. Heat at low heat using a microwave, a dehydrating oven, or a traditional oven.

A home dehydrator makes it easy and very effective. Just follow the instructions.

Conventional ovens work equally well if you monitor the temperature closely. If the temperature is too low, the herbs may lose their color and taste. The ideal temperature should be between ninety and one-hundred and ten degrees Fahrenheit. It should be maintained during the drying process. It is important to keep the oven door open. You should also check to make sure that the leaves and herbs are not being turned. The entire process may take as long as four hours.

A microwave oven works well for drying herbs in a small quantity. It is also more efficient. It is also much faster. Do not disregard the instructions. You could end up setting yourself ablaze if you do not follow them.

Wash the herbs well and dry them completely. Place the herbs between 2 sheets of paper towels. Microwave on the high setting between one and three mins. Turn the herbs once every thirty seconds. The herbs should dry evenly. Once they are dried, let them cool completely before placing them in a container.

You can remove all the leaves from their stems once they have cooled down. Keep them out of direct sunlight and in a dry, cool place. It is best to not crush the leaves as this can cause the flavor to lose its quality. Properly stored herbs will keep their great taste for upto a year.

Drying herb seed

The stems should be removed from the seed heads as soon the skins turn brown. Tie them together in groups, then place these small bundles in their paper bags. Once the seeds are dry shake them to separate their heads. Now rub the seeds gently with your fingers. You can also take out the chaff and hulls by placing them on a tray. The drying time for seeds is usually longer than that of leaves. If the seeds aren't completely dry, they could turn moldy.

Freezing Herbs

Frozen herb are not recommended for use in salads and garnishing. They work best when used as garnish in cooked food. This is the easiest way to preserve extra herbs and won't affect their flavor in any way.

You should first rinse the herbs. After rinsing your herbs, cut them into small pieces and place them in water-filled ice cubes. Once they have froze solid, transfer them into a container or bag. Then store them in the freezer. As you need, separate the cubes.

You can also blanch the leaves for a short time and then cool them down quickly in icewater. The herb leaves may now be stored in sealed plastic bags in the freezer.

Common Mistakes Made By New Gardeners

This is a common mistake made by novice herb gardeners. Here are some tips that will help you avoid making the same mistakes. These tips will ensure that you are able to grow and harvest your herbs quickly.

Instead of using artificial additives that can cause health problems, use fresh aromatic herbs. They are delicious and good for your health. The right herbs are able to transform any pasta sauce or enhance any dish. You can buy many fresh herb varieties at the market, but nothing is as satisfying as growing your own herbs. It doesn't really matter if your apartment is in the middle of the city or if you don't have a garden, you can still plant your own herbs indoors.

Remembering my first venture, I searched the Internet for advice but found the information too complex and overwhelming to be able to comprehend. It seems that it is geared towards high-end gardeners. This includes the soil's pH. I will now give you the details and basic information necessary to be a herb dummy. It will make it easy and keep you from falling for all the traps. Here are the things you need to avoid.

Growing herbs with seeds

My first recommendation is to purchase seedlings over seeds to grow herbs. If you are a novice, starter plants will give your confidence the boost you need. There are many things you can do wrong when growing seeds, especially as they develop from seeds into seedlings. These baby herbs can be bought in most grocery markets. You will be charged the same amount for your starter herb plant as you would for one packet. However, you can harvest many more herbs from one plant.

False Choice of Varieties

Some herbs can be more difficult than others. You don't want to start with something more delicate and difficult. Basil is the #1 choice for beginners due to a few reasons. Basil is a quick grower, so you will feel the sweetness of success within a matter of days. Basil will show you when it lacks moisture immediately. Your basil leaves will wilt. But if you water them well, they will recover well and you can continue to grow. Basil, like a canary at the bottom of a mine shaft, can help you decide how much water to provide for your plants.

Water your herbs the same way you water other houseplants

Most houseplants only need one large watering each week. Herbs on the other side are more delicate and require a lot of moisture. They are happy to receive a consistent, moderate amount of water, so it is important that you stick to this routine especially during the summer heat. Before adding soil, make sure that the bottom of your pots has at least one drainage hole. Sticking to this rule will ensure your plants are well-drained and won't be affected by overwatering.

Pruning too soon is not enough

Don't let your baby plant be considered too small for a haircut. Waiting for the leaves to grow more will not help you. Basil is the ideal herb to get started. Basil is a passionate grower. The stem can be removed right above a healthy set of leaves. This will stop your stem from growing and instead encourage two new, young stems to grow around it. If you don't cut the main stalk, it will grow taller and more heavily and eventually become a bush. The base of your plant should be about three to four feet above the ground. Keep a few solid leaves on your plants. When it has grown to four more inches, trim it again to about three inches beyond the first cut. After a few trimmings it will be enough to make enough aromatic basil leaves for the next pizza.

Avoiding the Wrong Leaves

You may think it is obvious to start harvesting the bigger leaves towards the base of your plant. Then, you can continue to grow the new tender leaves on the top. I fear you are wrong. The big, sturdy ones you shouldn't touch are the solar panels of your plant and provide the power that your herb grows. Your herb plant should be large enough for you to harvest the first harvest. Once that happens, pick at the top just as you would with pruning. Never trim beneath a set or leaves. Cut just above the foliage. This is exactly where the new growth happens. These tender leaves are the most flavorful. Your plant will continue to grow as the powerhouse at the base will continue to develop new stems.

Allowing the plants to become disorderly

Your plants will stay healthy by being pruned regularly. Some plants produce edible flower but you will need to prune them regularly if your intention is to harvest their leaves. This will encourage the plants grow their leaves.

Use of soil without nutrients

A garden that has had soil outside for a long period of time will eventually look old, grey, and very depressing. Soil that has been left outside for too long will look tired and grey. Plant your herbs in rich and healthy soil. You will see a return on your investment. I recommend you use good potting soil with good organic compost and used coffee grounds. The coffee grounds can be obtained at your local coffee shop free of charge. If you have them, add a little bit of crushed up egg shells. Miracle Grow works equally well as compost, however, it can be used in a more diluted form.

Falling into a Rut

The more you succeed at your endeavors, you'll become more passionate. Your first herbs will bring you great rewards, so take advantage of your passion and grow! Now that you have conquered the one herb, try other favorite herbs. My recommendation would be to go back to mint, rosemary, thyme, and oregano. They all make great additions to any kitchen and are relatively easy to grow. Do the same with rosemary as basil. If it does not develop, don't be alarmed. Remember that some plants respond better to pruning than others by producing more large leaves towards their base.

Avoiding the Wrong Kind of Herb

You bought a mint plant to make mint tea. When you go to purchase it, however, you find out that it's not the right kind of mint. There are many kinds of mint. Oregano comes also in two main varieties. You can choose from Mediterranean or Mexican, which is the most commonly found dried herbs shelf. My personal favorite is Mexican oregano. It works well in a spicy dish with beans or home-cooked tomatoes and is delicious with any other tomato dish. It is important to read labels carefully, as you might get a spearmint mint or apple mint rather than regular mint.

Invasive herbs

You should do your homework before you attempt to plant more than 1 type of herb in one container. Before you know it, your small mint plant might have grown to be a gigantic, taking over the whole container and killing everything else. Oregano can also be a voracious grower, and should therefore be grown in its very own container. I recommend planting these prodigious growers in a container dug into the soil to protect their roots. They could become a nuisance to their neighbors if they are not careful.

Chapter 5: Various Herbs & How To Use Them

Herbs have been used over the centuries for their incredible culinary and medicinal properties. Now, you might expect to find a complete collection of herbs with their different uses. I'm afraid it will prove impossible.

There are many varieties of herbs with medicinal and culinary properties. In fact, there are hundreds upon hundreds of schools and ideas on herbs and their use, with each having its own objectives and teachings. Each of these schools will have developed their own lists of the most effective herbs.

Medicinal Uses

However, there are many western herbs that are common in all parts of the world and most people find them very useful in daily life. There are herbs that can treat diseases and maladies as well as herbs with cosmetic properties. It doesn't matter if you need to get relief from a medical condition, or if you want to use natural products to improve your beauty routine, herbs can certainly help.

There are many schools in the world of herbs. The differences in cultures and histories of countries where herbs are most popular lie at the root of their greatest appeal. Chinese herbal medicines for healing rely on the energy and properties of the plants. Ayurveda however, originated in India and focuses on balancing all five of life's forces.

The western schools focus on these views and are based in part on the many traditions that exist in western countries (including the USA). They rely on both the curative properties and the synergistic effects of herbs in order to heal diseases.

Next, let me give you a short list of some commonly used herbs. I will then discuss the many ways that they can help improve your overall health and life in general. Before you decide to embark on any type of treatment, whether herbal or otherwise, it is important that you consult your physician. Because some herbs can interact negatively with other medications, it is important to inform your physician.

California Poppy

This beautiful, yellow flower, also known to be called a "flame flower", promotes relaxation. It is used to relieve anxiety and reduce depression. It is said to help with anxiety and tension.

Catnip

Make a cup of catnip tea to help you relax and let go of stress. Because it relaxes muscles that can cause cramps, it will help relieve menstrual symptoms. It can also relieve the symptoms of chronic, annoying cough.

Chamomile

Chamomile tea provides relief from upset stomachs by its calming effects. It will aid you to sleep as it acts as a mild stimulant.

Dandelion

It is considered a nuisance by many gardeners. However, there are many healing properties to it. It is an herb that can aid in digestion and boost the functioning your kidneys. This will cause an increase in your urine production which will aid in flushing out your urinary tract.

Dill

Dill is an antibiotic with anti-inflammatory & anti-viral qualities. Use this tonic to treat indigestion. Soon you will feel much better.

Echinacea

This plant's intense purple flower is well-known for its immune booster properties. Many people use it to boost their immune system and help them recover from illness. This combination can create an immune-boosting powerhouse.

Feverfew

Are you suffering headaches or severe migraines? This is the remedy. This herb has the ability to reduce the symptoms of migraines such as nausea, vomiting and light-sensitivity. The use of feverfew as an oral remedy for asthma, arthritis and dizziness is possible.

Garlic

This bulb is a wonderful herb that has been used for the treatment of colds and bacterial infections since ancient times. Include it in your daily diet and you'll boost your immune systems and get rid of many toxins.

Ginger

Another favorite, this little spicy root has been used amongst many other digestive conditions to treat indigestion and nausea. This will regulate the function and health of your digestive track.

Marijuana

Many people have tried marijuana to relieve pain. It will increase your appetite and alleviate nausea. It is also useful in treating glaucoma.

Peppermint

Many aromatherapists use mint to help patients feel better. Classical medicine frequently uses this herb for the treatment of digestive diseases. Mint is an herb with the greatest antioxidant power of all foods, and it can be used to treat many allergies. The menthol in this herb can relieve symptoms of colds. A cup of minty tea is the best choice.

Valerian

Valerian is great for those who have difficulty falling asleep at night. It acts as an effective natural sedative to decrease anxiety. The Californian Poppy can be used to make a stronger but gentle sedative.

Yarrow

If you have a serious cold or other inflammation, yarrow is a good choice. It is often used for the treatment of cramping and ulcers.

Culinary Uses

While this may seem obvious to you, many people don't know how to best use herbs in their cooking. If you are one among those people who is prone to grab the parsley and add it to every dish, then here are some guidelines to help you determine which herbs are most suitable for which dishes. I'll begin with meats.

Beef

Depending upon the type of beef dish, you can add any or all of these herbs: marjoram for soups and coriander, garlic, marjoram for salads, coriander, garlic, and thyme to almost any recipe. Sage and oregano are good options for tomato-based dishes.

Roast Beef

I love garlic and mustard and rarely prepare a roast if it isn't. But, you could also use rosemary oregano.

Chicken

I love rosemary and almost every chicken recipe. However, you can also add marjoram or garlic to your chicken recipe.

Fried Fish

Oregano works well with any fried seafood meal. Use sage, mustard and tarragon in your recipe.

Poached Fish Grilled

Fennel is my favorite herb for fish preparations this way. It has a delicate flavor. Coriander and thyme, both herbs that are great for this recipe, also work well.

Turkey

Try the following: rosemary, cumin basil, sage and thyme with your turkey

Pork

Pork is great with many herbs, such as rosemary and garlic, oregano and even marjoram.

Here's a list of dishes which include herbs that enhance their flavor. The most common herbs will be the ones I focus on, as the list of them is just too long.

Basil: tomatoes, salads, pasta dishes, peas.

Dill: cottage, cream cheeses. Also potatoes, tomatoes, pickles.

Bay leaf: Vegetarian dishes and all hearty foods such as soups, stews or tomato sauces.

Mint: jelly, teas. fruit salads. juices.

Marjoram is used in cheese, vegetable soups as well as stuffing and stews.

Oregano: Pastas, pizzas, tomato, aubergines, chilli, and vegetable dishes.

Rosemary: potatoes, cauliflower, zucchini, poultry stuffing.

Parsley: All vegetable, cheese, and egg dishes.

Thyme: Any type of vegetable soup, egg or bean soup, and all cheeses.

Sage: stuffings, pumpkin and butternut.

Tarragon can be used for green salads as well as cheese and egg dishes. It also makes it possible to make pickles, tomatoes, and other condiments.

Chapter 6: Every Journey Begins With The First Step

Picture yourself reaching out for a piece of fruit and taking one bite. For a more flavorful meal, grab some fresh herbs. You will be more satisfied if you prepare your own meals. It's not easy to put in the work and reap the rewards, but it is well worth it. The taste is also amazing. After you have tasted the fresh flavor of a fresh fruit and vegetable, you'll see why it is better than the grocery shop.

Many of us are in poor areas for gardening. It doesn't matter if it is winter 9 months out, or if you have extreme heat. You know the struggles of trying to grow a garden. It is not possible to grow in extremes of temperature, and it can be very difficult for our gardening plans to succeed.

Many people don't have the opportunity to have a backyard. We all know how precious space can be for those who live in apartments and large cities. Most of the time, outdoor space is not suitable for gardening.

Many people are now using indoor gardening to grow their gardens. The best part about indoor gardening is that it doesn't leave you to the will of the elements. You can now control your water, heating, and other critical factors. You can grow indoors any time of year, no matter your location. This makes it a great choice for virtually any area. Even if there is a healthy garden outside, it can be brought indoors to add some color and interest to your home.

Indoor gardening is also easy and very low-maintenance. All you need are some seeds (or pregrown plants), soil, a container, an appropriate location, and some time. Even a small windowill is enough for a couple of plants. Therefore, even the smallest of homes can grow plants. It's a great hobby for anyone, because it doesn't cost any money, time or space.

Indoor gardening generally can be divided into two main types. Hydroponics, and the more common container garden. Most people think of container gardening when they think of gardening. These are plants that are grown in containers with soil. This type is what we'll be focusing on because it's the easiest. Hydroponics requires more work and costs more, but we'll briefly mention it. A seasoned gardener might opt for this route but most people prefer to do container gardening.

LOCATION.

Your first and most important decision when starting a garden is, as with real estate. The basic need for light is something that most people know. However, there are many other factors that you should keep in mind. Each of the above factors are important for the overall health of your flower. You will ensure that your plants are healthy by spending some time planning ahead. Indoor gardening has many advantages.

You can choose the location and take care of the plants. This gives you an advantage as you can make changes to create the perfect atmosphere for your plants.

This section will focus on the essential things you need to keep in mind as you choose the best location to grow your garden. Each of these elements is important. After reading this section, you'll be able comprehend each point and be able make informed decisions regarding where to plant your plants. Let's review the top factors that you should consider when choosing your location for growing.

Selection Of Plants

While you're looking through these tips, it's important to consider what type of plant your goal is to grow. There are many requirements that plants may have, and you can often make generalizations. Vegetables are a good example. They need lots of light so you will need to prioritize them when you plant these plants. When you consider your location, these are the things that will help you choose the right plant for the right place. If you pick the wrong plant for your location, you will likely end up with plants that are not well-suited to the area.

Light

Lighting should be the main concern when choosing the best location for your garden. It is best to have a sunny, south-facing window. This will allow the plants to receive the maximum light. It is important to consider what plants you are growing. Not all plants require the same amount of light.

A little more shade, or even indirect light will be beneficial depending on the type and size of the plant. You will need to spend some time researching the light requirements for your plants.

Remember to consider the possibility for grow lights being used in lieu of natural lighting. Grow lights can be as effective and flexible as natural lighting, giving you more options for where to plant. This is especially important for those who lack natural light or have smaller gardens. Consider the placement of the lights when planning your garden space. The bulb should be at least 2 feet from the plant. It all depends on the kind of bulb and what heat it emits. LED lights have become very popular. Because of their low heat production, they are safer when placed near plants. Higher heat bulbs are better placed further away, as the heat could cause injury to the plant.

Last, be aware of the various levels of intensity that occur throughout the year. People who live in seasonal areas will notice that the sunlight is more intense during winter months. You might find that certain plants don't thrive during winter months. This means you'll either need to relocate them or supplement your lighting with grow lights.

Size

Another important thing to remember is the area you want to grow in. It depends on the kind of plants you are looking to grow, as well as how many. Not only do more plants take up more room, but each plant also has different requirements. Look for plants that are compatible with your space. While a windowill can be great for small herb plants, a tomato garden won't fit in the same spot.

Plants receive nutrients from soil roots. This means that plants will benefit from more space when they grow. A large amount of space is necessary for healthy root growth. Many plants start small but require large containers due their robust root system.

If you have limited space or wish to maximize it, vertical gardening is an option. A wire rack, or simple shelf, is a great option to add plants to a small space. These racks are inexpensive and will maximize your grow space. Remember to keep the lighting level in mind when you use a rack. In many cases, the higher levels will receive the most sunlight and block the lower ones a little.

Airflow

While this isn't usually an issue it's important to keep in mind that plants need carbon dioxide to survive. This is a normal process that occurs in most homes and shouldn't pose any problems. You won't need to worry if your plants live in an open, centrally located area of the home.

It is possible for your plants to be damaged if they are kept in a tight space, such as a small closet. A fan small enough to provide sufficient airflow is adequate if this happens. Keep it on a low setting to mimic the breeze. If you have small plants that are sprouting, high settings can cause problems, especially for those with weak stems. Most people won't be concerned about this, however, special gardens with enclosed areas might.

Temperature

Although plants are typically resistant to large temperature changes, it is possible for them to be damaged by drastic temperature changes. This is more important for plants that grow in tropical environments such as fruits. You can minimize this risk by growing indoors, as long as your home remains relatively consistent in temperature. But there are still things to consider.

Keep your plants safe from high temperatures. These include air vents or heaters. Anything too hot or cool will cause problems. These lights should not be left too close to plants. LEDs offer beginners one less thing.

Drafty windows in winter are another source of temperature problems. You can make your plants die if you leave them in an area where cold air blasts at them. This can cause plants to become stunted or even die. Make sure that they are kept at the same temperature.

Also consider the ideal temperature range you want for your plants. The average indoor temperature in most homes is fine for most plants. Some tropical plants require more humidity or temperatures. If your goal is to grow more exotic plants, keep this in mind.

If you are just starting out with your garden, I would recommend that you start small. Even though it may be tempting, you should not rush to buy too many plants, especially if there are large empty spaces around your home. Learn how to take care of plants by starting small. For new gardeners, although it is not difficult to do, it can seem daunting at times. Many people go out to buy plants, only to find that they have a lot left over. Start small, and you can grow from there. The best thing about gardening is that it can be a rewarding hobby for a lifetime.

Containers are the home of the plant

Once you have settled on a spot, you need to decide how you are going to house them. Indoor gardening is a wonderful way to have fun with creative containers. This allows for a lot more freedom. However, there are important things to consider when choosing a pot. We will be looking at different options for container choices and how to pick the right one.

There are literally hundreds to choose from for housing your plant. If you're creative, this is the perfect occasion to let your imagination run wild. There are lots of pre-made, budget-friendly options available if you're not a creative person. We'll look at some of these more popular choices, but let's start by looking at what makes a container great for indoor gardening.

Choose the right size

Use the information you have gathered in the previous steps to determine how big a container is needed. This is determined according to the root size, growth behavior, and other factors. Some plants develop deep roots, while others, such lettuce, produce shallower and wider root systems. It is important to choose a container which will fit your plant well and allow for sufficient space for growth.

Chives, for example are a relatively small root plant. This means that you can grow them in a very small pot. You will often see them growing on small windowsills.

Many plants will not grow in tiny containers. This can, however, limit their growth. This can be a good way to limit the growth of large plants, but it can also make it difficult for them to reach the right size to produce fruits or vegetables. It's best that you start with the right container. As your plant grows, you may want to experiment with different size containers to see what happens.

Drainage Holes

Drainage holes are another important aspect. Commercial pots usually have drainage holes along the sides and bottom. It allows for water drainage and helps to minimize the negative effects of overwatering. As we have already mentioned, standing water is harmful to your plants and can cause root disease. It is possible to kill your plants by standing water. This is the biggest problem novice gardeners will face.

While you can use any container with drainage, it is more difficult and not recommended for most gardeners. We'll be looking at tips and tricks later in this section to help you avoid standing water in soil.

Clay pots are a popular choice for gardeners. They help reduce the amount of sitting water. Clay pots trap water and prevent overwatering. We'll be more detailed about them soon, but they merit an extra mention here.

In many cases, it is possible to create your own drainage holes. You can drill through plastic materials, making it easy to place drainage holes in the bottom. It's not possible to do this with all containers, like glass. However, it can help a lot.

Spill Prevention

There are often small holes in your container so be ready for spillage. This is typically water, soil or other small plant debris which slips through these drainage holes. Most containers include a tray at the bottom to collect this type of runoff. These are recommended if you don't want dirt or water to all over your home. It is not necessary, but it is something to consider if maintaining a tidy grow area.

You should leave enough space for drainage rocks

Another common practice involves adding rocks or gravel to the bottom. This gives water a direct route and is similar to the holes mentioned above. It is a good way to avoid root rot and overwatering.

Add rocks to bottoms of containers with no drainage holes. This will give water a place to go so the roots don't sit in it.

Mason jars are a good container. However, it is best to fill the top inch with small stones. While this can also be used for other containers, it's not as important for containers with holes that allow water escape.

Let's move on to the common types of containers!

Clay Pots

The clay fired pottery pot is one of many options available for indoor growth. These pots can be bought at most hardware stores for very cheap. These pots are sometimes called terracotta.

They are not durable and will crack if dropped or exposed at freezing temperatures. They can also dry out quickly due to the fact that clay whisks away water. You should water these pots regularly. They make great choices for low-water plants like the cacti.

This pot is a good choice for beginners. This pot has a whisking function that actively reduces the likelihood of gardeners drowning. Many store-bought pots come with drainage holes that make them easy to start.

The clay can also be painted or decorated, making them a wonderful choice for creative people.

Clay pots can be a good choice for beginner gardeners. When purchased from a retail store, clay pots are typically ready for planting without any additional effort. Although they might not be as popular as other container options they are sturdy, inexpensive, and require little maintenance.

Glazed Ceramic

Another excellent option for containers is ceramic. They are just as easy-to-find as clay and are more resistant than clay to cold temperatures when left outside in winter. They come in a variety sizes and colors, however they are more expensive than the standard clay pot.

These will most likely come with drainage holes. This saves you the time and effort of making them. These plants will not have the same whisking powers as clay and you will have to be more careful about how much water you use.

These pots are great for those who wish to create a decorative container with minimal effort. Ceramic pots can be found in many styles.

Wooden

Wooden containers bring a natural appearance to your garden. They look great, but can only last for a few years before they need to be replaced. A wooden container may need an inner lining in order to keep dirt from seeping.

Wooden containers are great if you want to keep your space natural and rustic. They are also available in many sizes so you can easily find one for your space.

Most cases will require you to seal them annually to extend their life span. If they start to rot, you may need to re-seal them. They should also be able to drain properly. Before you plant, make sure that the container is completely drained.

If it takes longer, you might want to make drainage holes.

Plastic

Plastic containers are popular and very affordable, just like clay. They can last for a long time, and they can take abuse. They do not retain water like clay. Be careful with watering and make sure you don't overwater.

Plastic can be used in many ways that clay cannot, with the exception of the need to whisk water. Plastic is also available in a wide range non-standard shapes and designs that allow you to have fun. Plastic is easy to modify if there aren't any holes, or if you need to.

Mason Jar

Glass mason-jars, which are smaller than standard containers for growing vegetables, are an example. A mason-jar should be topped with a few inches of gravel for drainage. This is important because most mason containers don't have drainage holes.

This container is too small for some plants, but it's a good starting container. It also makes a nice talking point. This container can be used for small herbs or flowers.

Other Non-standard

With sufficient care, you can use almost any container as a home for plants. People have succeeded with using old boxes and other items from their home. This is a chance to be imaginative and create something original and exciting.

People have even used coffee mugs from the past to grow their plants.

It doesn't really matter what container you use as long there is adequate drainage and sufficient room for your plants. This is it. However, don't make a hasty decision. A poor container will only make your gardening journey more difficult. For beginners clay pots may be your best choice. However, if clay isn't an option, it's possible to go wrong with clay.

Soil and Nutrients

Soil is what your plants use to get their nutrients. It is crucial for healthy plants. It is also a problem for indoor gardeners because it does not change. In indoor gardens, the only thing that can replenish the nutrients is you. This typically requires some form of fertilizer, or compost to be added. We'll get to that shortly enough. Let's begin by choosing the best soil.

This section will teach you how to maximize the soil in your garden. Also, learn about fertilizing and how to compost your soil to keep it nutrient-rich.

Dirt Vs.

Gardeners are often asked the following question: What is the difference in soil and dirt?

The basic answer is that the medium must have a high nutritional content. Dirt is generally defined as soil with no nutrients. If you pick up a handful dirt, it will not clump and likely have no microorganisms. It's not the right place for plants.

But soil is richer in nutrients than it is in micro-organisms. A handful soil will clump together easily and retain more water than normal dirt. The presence of red worms is a sign that your soil is nutrient rich. In nutrient poor soil, such creatures are unlikely to survive.

A bag of soil can be a great option to start your garden. These are highly nutritious and make a great starting place for your plants. Two main reasons it is not advisable for you to get dirt from outside are:

1. The soil may not contain enough nutrients to support your plants.

2. It could have harmful parasites that you don't know about. These parasites will likely cause problems for your plants. You can save money by buying a bag full of potting dirt. The bag doesn't necessarily have to cost a lot, as many varieties can be just as good for growers. But, make sure you buy soil marked for

potting. Soil for outdoor garden beds does not have the same drainage properties as potting soil and is not suitable for containers.

Most of these pre-packaged organic soils are not intended to be used for long periods. The soil is organic material. It will naturally decompose with time. The following are signs.

* The soil compresses and appears to be almost settled. The soil will appear less light-colored and fluffy. This will cause the soil to become tight around the roots and deprive the plant of oxygen.

* You may notice that drainage is slow and soil drying takes longer. In some cases, there might be standing water. This hinders the plants' ability to get the water they need, and increases the likelihood of root-rot.

Salt and mineral build up. You'll notice whiter stripes around clay pots. This is the result of minerals and salt leaking into the container. This is not a problem if you have a small amount, but excessive amounts can fry and kill the root system of your plant.

You can avoid this by re-potting your plants at least once a year. It is as easy as taking the plants out of their containers and washing them with new soil. This will ensure your plants have enough nutrients and water to keep growing.

It is important to thoroughly wash pots when repotting, especially if you have left them outside. This prevents potential problems with pests such as transplanting bugs and other parasites.

You can keep your soil nutrient fresh by correct fertilizer use. While it's a good idea for plants to be repotted every other year, fertilizer can help keep them fresh between repottings. It is also our next topic.

Types of soil

Let's discuss soil types briefly as there might be some you are unfamiliar with. The majority of plants will grow well in store bought potting dirt, but some plants require different soil. Succulents, by contrast, prefer coarser soils that are 1/3 sand. They also drain quickly. The soil type and plant will be easier to maintain.

You may also come across a variety potting soil that is specific for tomato plants like tomato potting earth. These are excellent options, since they provide the right nutrients for optimal growth. These aren't necessarily necessary. Normal potting soil should work. Some plants, such as succulents and cacti, need more rapidly draining soil.

Fertilizer and Organic Compost

Important for healthy plants is making sure they have enough nutrients. The majority of potting soil that you buy in stores is packed with nutrients. But, over time, these nutrients will start to run out. This will mean that you will need some assistance. If the soil isn't full of nutrients, it can cause your plants to die. Good fertilizer application can bring some nutrients back to your soil. It will also save you the effort of repotting every so often.

Let's talk first about store-bought, premade fertilizer. These are great as they are convenient, fast, and affordable ways to add lots of nutrients to your soil. However, there are some important things to keep in your mind.

There is no dispersal

In the outdoors, fertilizer will naturally diffuse into the soil around it and spread throughout the gardens. A plant can take only what it needs while this happens and then allows the rest to be dispersed throughout the soil.

However, this is not true in an indoor container. The soil contains all the nutrients that you have put in. There is no room for water to filter through. The plant can be killed if too much fertilizer is used, especially if the fertilizer is chemical-based. A general rule of thumb is to reduce the amount you use by 1/4 for smaller containers.

This reduces fertilizer use, but still ensures that the plant has enough nutrients to survive. Mix equal parts fertilizer and water to get the desired concentration.

You shouldn't fertilize too often. This will depend on your plant. On average, fertilizing once every few months should be sufficient. You should be aware of this as some plants go dormant over the winter. You don't generally need to fertilize your plants during this time of dormancy as they are not receiving the usual amount nutrients.

Go Organic

Organic fertilizers are also recommended when indoors. This prevents the introduction of potentially harmful chemicals to your home and helps reduce the risk of fertilizer shocking plants. A good organic fertilizer will perform just as well as one that contains chemicals. Organic fertilizers are more expensive than chemical fertilizers.

Slow Release or Water-Soluble

There are many fertilizers on offer, but indoor use is the best. The most popular are water-soluble and slow release.

Water-soluble fertilizers mix right in your watering pot and then add to the water. This allows for you to have complete control over the amount you feed your plants. It also gives you the ability to adjust feeding times to best suit your plants' needs. It makes it simple to reach your desired level, simply use less fertilizer/more water to lower the concentration.

Slow-release fertilizers are added to the soil. They are protected with a special protective shell which leaches the fertilizer into soil. They are durable and easy to store, so they can be used for many months. They can be used sparingly in terms of fertilizer. This reduces the chance of plants being shocked by too much.

Compost

Comporium is the foundation of any discussion on feeding plants. Compost is made from decomposing matter. This could be anything, from apple cores to newspaper. These nutrients are what plants love and help to make compost. Additionally, you can make your own compost from household waste. This is a cost-effective way to fertilize your garden without compromising nutrients. Compost can be made from all-natural materials, so it offers all the benefits and affordability of organic fertilizer.

The smell can be a problem when composting indoors. The smell of compost, which is made up of decaying matter, can be quite unpleasant. There are many options to reduce this unpleasant smell. Let's see how we can get started with simple but effective compost. This will not make your house smell like garbage.

First, select a container. It is important to determine where your compost container will go. You will need to choose a container that is suitable for it. Containers can be of any size, but it is important to drill holes in their bottoms and to have some way to catch dirt. Plastic bags available in most shops are great for this, if there is enough space.

Once you have picked your container, location and ingredients, it's the time to add them. Important: Keep it at 2 parts brown for 1 part green.

The following brown items can be found:
* Newspapers
* Magazines
* Wood Shavings
* Dead Leaves
* Saw Dust

Green items Include:
* Fruit Waste
* Coffee ground
* Grass Clippings
* General Food Waste
* Tea Bags

Follow the below parts to ensure you stay on track

The smell. The best practice is to hide any food substances in the "brown," which will help mask any odors. If the smell starts to bother you, increase the amount of "brown", to favor "brown". These items are not odourless and can mask the smell of food waste. If the process is properly done, there shouldn't be any unpleasant odors.

The compost should be turned every few days. This not only keeps the smell down but also encourages healthy compost growth. Once the compost has turned a deep brown color and you cannot tell what it contained, it's ready to go!

Use the compost by simply sprinkling it over the soil. Then, work it in a little. Composter doesn't need any harsh chemicals. It won't damage your plants if it is added to too much soil.

The last thing to do is not include any animal droppings. These items can make the compost unfriendly, attract unwanted pests, create unpleasant stench, and cause a lot of problems. It is better to avoid them. Make sure your compost is made of plant-based material.

Chapter 7: What To Feed?

The type of flower you grow will affect how you feed your plant. Some plants are more hungry than others, and may need more frequent food. Some plants don't need to be fertilized at all. It's essential to spend some time learning about your plants to figure out how often they should be fertilized.

However, most plants only require a light feed every 4-8 weeks. Most plants respond well to these feedings.

A final note. Plants will often stop growing or become less productive in winter. This is typically caused by a decrease in sunlight. The plants will see this as an indication of slower growth indoors. This means that your plants will need less nutrients so you don't have as many fertilizers. This is dependent on the particular plant, but in most cases you can fertilize twice as often without any adverse effects.

Lighting the Way

As we all know, lighting is an essential aspect of healthy plants. Good lighting is key to beautiful and healthy plants. You can see the difference in their health and appearance. In this section, we will examine all things light and show you how to provide the right lighting for your plants.

Indoor gardening has two light sources: the sun, and grow lights. The sun is simple, a large windows is a great friend for gardeners. It's also completely free so it's worth considering. An alternative source of light is to install artificial grow lights. These lights can provide natural light, and they are a good option. However, installing artificial lights can be quite difficult. There are many options for intensity and types of artificial light, so it may be confusing at first to find the one that is right for your needs. You don't have to worry about it, as we will be going in-depth on the different types later in this chapter.

Know Your Plants

It is important to determine what lighting your plants require before you start to figure out how best to light them. Some plants need 12+ hour direct sunlight. Others will wilt under the same conditions. It's crucial to learn about your plants and ensure that they receive the care they need.

It is generally true that plants that you intend on eating require the most lighting. This applies to vegetables, fruits, and herbs. These plants are most likely to need 8+ hours light. If you do not, your growth will be stunted. However, these plants might not need a lot of light. It is important to fully understand the needs of each flower.

But many indoor plants can do without much light, or even significant shade. A peace lily, for instance, can actually wilt in too much lighting. This just shows the range of lighting requirements for plants. The most important point here is that light requirements vary among plants. Be aware of this and plan accordingly.

Natural Light

Natural light is the best option for gardeners. This is also the easiest option because it doesn't require much setup. The sun is available for your use so you should get as much light as possible.

As you can see, plants have different lighting needs. Therefore, make sure that the area in which you are planting is getting enough natural light. It is also important to understand that the intensity of light in many places decreases in the winter. This means that areas that get sufficient sunlight in summer don't receive enough light during winter. Note this and adjust accordingly.

Other than that, you don't really have much to do. All you need to do is make sure your plants get enough light. You need to begin looking into grow light options. That's where the real difficulty begins.

Sunlight Facing Directions

It's common to see that a south-facing window is the best for gardening. This is because south facing windows are the best for getting the most light. However, all windows will allow light into your home. Understanding the differences in light levels is crucial. These estimates are general and may not be accurate depending on where you live. Light levels can be affected by obstructions like trees and other objects.

North

The north-facing window doesn't get much sunlight, but it does get enough in-direct light. These windows are good for plants who need plenty of light but dislike the intensity of direct sunlight.

South

Windows that face south get the most sunlight. In many cases they will be able to receive almost full sunlight throughout the day. This is the best place for light heavy plants such fruits and vegetables.

East

East-facing windows are great for plants that need both direct and indirect sunlight. The morning will typically have some direct sunlight, while the rest of day will be less intense.

West

Similar to the east, west facing windows offer a mix between direct and indirect light. You'll see mostly in-direct daylight most of day, with some direct lighting towards the end of the night.

Ordinal

There are also a variety of in-between directions, like Northwest or Southeast. These directions usually combine several of their constituent directions. A southeast facing windows will receive some in-direct sunlight, but a lot of direct sunlight. Direct sunlight will be much less than the window that faces south, but far more than one that faces east.

How to Get Started With Lights

Indoor grow lighting is a great way of providing additional or replacement sunlight to your plants. The lights behave just like the sun. However the amount of light they receive and the distance it's from the plant will influence how long it lasts.

Here are some tips to help you choose the right type of light for your garden.

Be careful with your lights

Depending on what lights you use (if applicable), they can get extremely hot. The lights can heat up to the point that they can burn your plants. You will want to allow between 12"-24" for your plants and the light fixtures in most cases. These lights will be able to cover the greatest area and avoid any heat hazards. Incandescent bulbs can emit a lot, but they are quite energy efficient.

LED lighting can be a good option for beginning growers. They are simple, affordable, and extremely efficient. They don't produce a lot of heat so they can be located closer than incandescents.

Understanding Light Wavelengths

The wavelengths of light and their effects on the plants are important things to remember. Different wavelengths of light stimulate the plants differently, and different lighting sources emit light at different intensities. In many cases, the best results will be achieved with a combination of different wavelengths. Here are a few wavelengths that you need to pay attention to when purchasing lights.

Red: Promotes flowering.

Blue: Promotes leaf growth

White: A mixture from all types of wavelengths

Each one of these has different uses so you may have to mix them up depending on what your goals are.

Incandescent Lights

The standard incandescent lamp is the most basic. These are your basic lightbulb. They get hot. These will damage your plants if they are placed too close to the plant.

Incandescent bulbs are not recommended for beginners as they can be very difficult to use and inefficient. However, they emit red wavelengths which can promote blooming plants. They complement the bright blue light of fluorescent lights quite well, as you can see. If you are interested in using them, 1/3 of an incandescent should be your starting point.

Fluorescent Lighting

These light bulbs come in two main varieties: the larger tubes and the smaller bulbs. The tubes are great to cover large areas while the bulb can be used to target specific plants.

The bulbs are also very cost-effective due to their low energy consumption.

Fluorescent bulbs are less expensive than older incandescent bulbs. They also release less heat, so they can be placed closer to plants that require brighter light without worrying overheating.

Fluorescent lighting emits a lot if blue light. Make sure you look for one labeled "full Spectrum". This will ensure sufficient light is available to encourage paper growth for all types plants.

LED Lights

Another option for growing is LED lighting. They come in many colors. Because there is a wide range of lights, it's important to select the one that you need for your specific purpose. This will ensure that they are able to produce the right wavelengths for plant growth. The wavelengths of many common LED lights aren't correct, so ensure you choose the best lighting.

High Intensity Dispcharge (HID).

High Intensity discharge (HID) lights are the last options for lighting. These lights are mainly used for large commercial farms and not by recreational growers. While you won't likely come across it, it's something that's worth knowing.

Placement in Light

To expose the entire plant evenly, the light should be directed overhead. This isn't always possible. Even with sun, there will be times when one side gets more light than others.

You can rotate the plant to face the sun by turning it upside down. You may notice that the plant can bend towards the light at times. This can lead, if not rotated correctly, to a weaker stem that could cause more complications. A simple rotation allows you to expose the sides of your plant and keeps it straight.

Timers for Light

While plants do require light, there are also times when they need to be darkened. Respiration, which is the opposite to photosynthesis, is a process that plants go through. Respiration, unlike photosynthesis does not require sunlight. This means that it can be done in the dark. It is important that plants get the same light and dark cycles as they get in nature.

If the sun is the primary source of your light, then it is done for you. Just leave the plant to go dark at night. This will work fine for most common houseplants.

A light-timer is an easy way to use grow lights. To control when the lights are on or off, you can set the timer for specific periods. Light timers cost very little and are great for gardeners who forget to turn the lights on or off.

You want to create a similar environment as the plant would like in nature. Try to mimic the natural habitat that your plants live in and provide them with similar conditions.

Common Lighting Issues

Let's conclude with a discussion about lighting problems.

The problem of leaves browning or wilting can sometimes be caused by poor lighting. This could be caused by too many direct sunlight or grow lights that are too close or hot. You need to be aware that this could also be a watering issue.

Plant Bending: This happens when there is more light on one side. Plants will often bend towards light. This can cause weak stems, as well as future growth problems. You can simply rotate the plant every few day to maintain a consistent light level.

My plants won't produce or flower: This is often due in large part to the lack of enough light. While some fruits and vegetables may grow well under low lights, many won't grow enough to be edible. In this case, increase the amount of light that is given to the plant. You might try increasing the intensity of the light, or adding more red to grow lights.

All About Water

Watering is often one of most challenging parts of growing plants. Watering is an essential part of growing plants. However, it can be overwhelming to know just how much. Watering problems are the number one reason indoor gardens produce less-than-ideal plants. This section will cover how to properly water plants, how not to overwater, and what to do if you make common watering errors.

While every plant has a unique water requirement, there are some common rules that can be followed for all plants. This chapter will examine these general ideas. At the end of this chapter, we'll highlight some plants that are popular and address their water requirements.

One is that plants grown indoors dry out much faster than outside plants. It is not possible for indoor plants to spread their roots to find additional water. Although an outdoor plant can search for water, indoor plants need to be watered regularly by a professional gardener. It doesn't have rain water, so the only water your plant receives is from yourself.

The container does not allow excess water to run off. The water can drain outside through the soil, but inside a container it doesn't. Avoid overwatering. It is possible to prevent overwatering by providing adequate drainage support in the container.

Most plants need water when the soil is just dry. This is a general rule of thumb that can be used for most plants. Give the soil just a little bit of water, about one inch deep. Only water when it is completely dry. This is a good way to reduce overwatering.

These are general guidelines, so it may not work for all plants. However, it is important to fully understand your plants' needs. Each plant has its own unique watering needs so make sure to keep this in mind when creating a watering plan.

How Much Water Do You Need?

There are many factors that affect how much you should be watering your plants. There are several factors that influence how much water you should give your plants. These include its size, pot material, and plant itself. A larger plant may require more water. As a rule of thumb, soil should not be completely saturated. However, soil should not be covered with water. If the soil is saturated with water through its drainage holes, it has had enough water. You can then stop watering.

Let's take a closer look at what factors can affect the amount of water that your plant needs.

Plant Age

Plants in rapid growth or budding need more energy and water than plants that are old or dormant. To aid in their growth, make sure you give growing plants a little extra water. The reverse is true. Older plants are more likely not to require as much water as you give them and will be less inclined to sit in the water if you add too much. Check your soil regularly to make sure it isn't drying out and water it when it is.

Time of the Year

Winter brings a slower rate of growth for plants. This is especially true when plants receive natural sunlight. As plants grow less, they will require less water. Many plants experience periods of dormancy, even indoors. In these cases, less is always more because the plants will need to take in less water. As it is very easy to water the soil too much, make sure to test it before adding water.

Humidity

Plants living in extremely humid places will need less water. If you are worried about overwatering but notice the leaves becoming weaker, spray them with a spray and mist them lightly. This can give your plant some energy without adding more water to the soil.

How to determine if there are any issues?

Unfortunately, signs of both under and overwatering are often very similar. Wilting leaves is often the first sign. If you notice that your leaves are becoming wilted or discolored, then take some soil with you and test it to see if the soil is dry or saturated. This will tell you where the problem is.

Another sign of water overflow is:

* Leaves falling off
* Stunted Growth
* Discoloration

These are signs to look out for, but don't panic. You won't lose your plant if you water it incorrectly. Simply identify which problem you are having, and then give or withhold water until the problem is solved. If you check your plants on a regular basis, you should be able detect and correct any issues before they become serious.

It's not hard to water your plants, even though it can seem difficult to do for beginners. For most plants, the soil test will be your best option for keeping them healthy. For most people, getting into the habit is easy. Many plants die due to neglecting to water.

Plant watering should be part of your daily routine. It might be a good idea to check the plants you have while the coffee is being brewed in the morning. After a while you'll become familiar with the proper amount of water and be able to care for your plants like a pro.

It all depends on the Plant

I wanted to emphasize that all of these are general guidelines and that it is best to learn more about each plant. Many plants have specific requirements for watering care. Failure to comply with them can result in a decrease in their growth.

Cacti such as succulents or cacti can be watered twice a week. This is a vast improvement on the daily waterings required for many fruits and vegetables.

The important thing is to get to know your plants and plan for their watering. Doing so will make your plants more susceptible to failure.

Pruning Your Plant

Pruning is an important aspect of gardening, yet it's often overlooked. Although it can be scary to cut into a plant's roots, it is actually very easy and beneficial. This section will be very brief but will discuss the most important aspect of pruning your plants and what it does for them.

Regular pruning is beneficial for all plants. The cutting back of some plants can actually help them grow. Although it might seem ironic, pushing back can actually help the plant grow larger.

A healthy plant will also be free from pests. Pests can be spread to plants' healthier parts if the dead or dying parts become infested. To prevent bugs from getting hold of your plant, you need to eliminate problem areas. Although they are less likely indoors, you shouldn't underestimate the power of their determination to kill your plants.

Pruning is an excellent way to maintain a healthy plant. It's easy to reduce the size of a plant that grows too large for you. Bonsai are a perfect example. There is an art and science to maintaining bonsai trees.

Sometimes it is hard to know when to prune or cut a plant. The plants are not always killed if they are harvested incorrectly. It can cause smaller crop sizes or lower flower numbers for a short time, but the plant is likely going to survive. Indoors, it's even more likely that the plant will survive a sudden freeze. So don't worry if things go wrong.

Pruning should be done with sharp, clean tools. You are basically exposing the plant to potential infections by cutting into its skin. It is important to clean your tools so that your plants are healthy.

General purpose pruning is best done in late winter, prior to the plants' growing season. If you do it too often, unopened buds could be removed and the plants' growth may be stunted. Don't forget to take care of your plants for aesthetic, sizing and general maintenance. It is important to regularly remove any dying or damaged parts. The risk of dead leaf budding is low so it should be done all year. If you intend to harvest later, make sure not to remove budding or growing stems.

If you notice pests on your plants, you should also trim the infected sections. This can prevent the pests spread and help maintain the health of the rest. You may have to sacrifice a small amount, but you can save the whole. This only works if the pests are caught early. Later we will discuss more ways to fight pests.

It is much simpler to harvest fruits, veggies, herbs. It is possible to still prune your plants to keep them in order, but you must only harvest the edible part of the plant when it is ready. It depends on the species of plant as well as your personal tastes.

Pruning: What to Avoid

Here are some tips to avoid. When pruning or harvesting, be sure to not cut too close to the stem or into the root. Pruning the plant is about cutting back, but not killing it. It is possible to be sure that your plant will grow back happy and healthy if the roots are left intact.

You don't want be too meticulous when pruning. A little bit is fine, but be mindful that you're only taking out small pieces of the plant every time.

Pruning is an essential part of plant growth and is relatively easy. While most gardeners are afraid to cut back their plants a little bit, in most cases you won't cause any damage. Because indoor plants are protected from all the elements, any excess pruning is unlikely to cause permanent harm. A little pruning can help your plant remain healthy and look good.

Pest Control

Unwanted pests can be a problem, and gardening is no exception. They are generally insects that can kill or damage your plants. This section will show you how to avoid pests and what to do if you find them.

You can greatly reduce the chance of infestation by following some easy steps. Pest control is not difficult. The old saying is "A good defense is the best offense." You can avoid the problem by taking preventive actions before the bugs arrive.

While indoor gardening does reduce the likelihood of pest infestations, it doesn't mean that they won't be an issue. There are still plenty of ways for pesky bugs that can attack your plants.

You are at greater risk if you allow your plants to be outside all the time or if you grow them outdoors but keep them inside during winter. These situations will make it more difficult to spot pests and you will need to monitor your plants closely.

We've got enough information. Let's now look at some ways you can prevent your plants from becoming pests.

Monitor Daily

It is important to keep your plants in check as often as possible to avoid an infestation. The first defense against these pesky creatures is to do a quick spot-check and check for any signs of infestation every day. This can be done easily if the plants are already being inspected to check for any signs of bugs.

The bugs are the most obvious indicator. Other signs can include discoloration and holes in the leaves or other damage. Make sure you check the undersides of all leaves. Common bugs cluster on the leaves' bottoms. Catching bugs early will make it easier to get rid of them.

It is important to monitor your plants closely in order to avoid pests. It's very rare for large infestations in a short time so it's possible to catch them before they become serious. As you might have guessed, it's easier to deal a few bugs than with large numbers.

Clean containers

Always wash all new containers thoroughly with warm soapywater before putting your plants in them. This is especially important if the container was purchased in a location that houses many plants. This includes hardware stores big and small, especially if the containers are stored outdoors in a garden section. All unwanted visitors can be removed with a quick wash using warm soapywater.

This is especially important for plants that are moved outside during the summer months. The containers should be washed before being brought back inside. This will prevent any bugs or eggs from sticking to the plants during summer.

Dead Leaves and Branches Must Be Removed As Soon as Possible

You can keep bugs away by monitoring the health and condition of your plant. You can trim dead or dying plants if you notice them. This applies to any dead leaves and stems found in your soil. Many insect species will thrive on a weak plant. These pruning methods will help you cut your plant back safely.

Common Pests

Here are some common indoor pests to watch out.

White Flies

Look out for black sticky film, which looks almost like mold. As they age they will appear like small, white flying insects. They will fly into the atmosphere if disturbed. They consume nutrients from plants and cause stunted or weak growth.

Aphids

Although they are most often green, they also come in other colors. They tend to cluster on the leaves' underside, so check there. They secrete an sticky substance that can attract more insects, like ants. They also feed off the plant, causing the leaves of the plant to wilt as well as general health problems for the entire plant.

Scale

On the stem, or the underside of the leaf, small and brown clusters form. Sometimes, they resemble small shells more than insects. As they can hide on branches, they can be difficult for people to see. The brown color allows them to blend in with plants quite easily so ensure you give your plant's roots a keen eye to avoid this pest going unnoticed.

Mealy bugs

They are fluffy and pale white and resemble cotton or the remnants a dandy, lion. They can be found everywhere, but usually they will be under the leaves first. A larger infestation is likely to be spotted elsewhere.

Spider Mites

These pests are too small to see with a magnifying glasses. If you notice leaf discoloration, it is usually a sign of their prior history. As their numbers increase, you may also see fine webbing appearing between the branches and leaves of your plants. This is almost like a spider's web. They are not an insect, but a species of arachnid.

I have an infestation. What now?

Now you know that you have pests. It is time to eradicate them. The solution to your problem will vary, as with everything. Let's have a look at solutions for common bugs.

Resolve the Problem

If you are lucky enough not to have an infestation, it may be possible to just remove the affected areas. You can remove an infestation that is limited to a particular area of the plant. The infestation can spread very quickly so it is best to be on the lookout for them early.

Beneficial bugs

Some bugs are beneficial to your garden. Common ladybug is a well-known "beneficial insect". Ladybugs keep pests from entering your garden. You can add them to your garden as an natural insect repellant. They don't cause any harm to your plants. It's best not to disturb them if you find them naturaly as they can attract more dangerous pests.

SoapyWater

Simply mix a bit of dish detergent with water in an easy-to-make spray bottle to create a natural repellent. This mixture has been shown not only to repel some types of bugs but also safe for your plants. It's also quick and easy to make. This is a good step to make if you have any bugs.

It is generally recommended that you start this on a small part of the plant. This prevents adverse reactions from occurring on a smaller portion of the plant. Once you are satisfied that the mixture is safe, you can use it on your entire plant.

Natural Pesticides

If soapy tap water is not enough, you can try natural pesticides. They have been proven effective in keeping bugs away. These are products such a neem and neem oils that are made from plants with natural pesticide qualities. You will need to choose the right one for your bug type. You can get rid of mealybugs with the above neem-oil. There are also other repellents to be used for different types of pests.

Don't panic. Do some research on the pest type to find the best way out. It is not difficult to eradicate most bugs. Your plants will return to their full potential with just a little bit of effort.

Chapter 8: Plant Specifics

Let's review some care tips after we've discussed all the main points that you need to know in order to start a gardening venture. We'll be applying all of what we've just learned, and going over specific care instructions for some popular plants. Below are some examples of common plants to help you get started growing them, as well as the details for how to do so.

Herbs

The beauty of herbs is that they can be grown indoors. They are an excellent choice because many herbs are hardy and can take some abuse. They can be difficult to kill, so even the most inept gardeners can still grow them.

There are many kinds of herbs. The care instructions can be very varied. However, plants need light that lasts at least six hours and moderate water. There is one great thing about herbs: their size. Many herbs can thrive in small pots, which makes them perfect for window sills and other small spaces. Let's now look at some popular herbs which you can immediately start growing.

Chives

Chives make a wonderful choice for growing as they can be used to create many different recipes and also have a delicious flavor. There are two types, the onion chives (common garlic chives) and the onion chives (or onion chives). They are both easy to care for, but they have a different taste. The difference can be easily identified by looking at the names.

Chives require 6-8 hours in the sun to lighten. A grow light can be used to supplement the light provided by natural sources. The chives will still thrive with less light, just not as fast.

Indoor plants of chives need to be watered only when the soil is dry. They are also fond of humid environments.

Water misting can be used to help maintain their moisture and prevent them from becoming too dry.

Research has shown that the smell of chives repels pests. The strong garlic and onion scents of chives are enough to protect them from pests. Chives are not commonly targeted by pests. The likelihood of pests targeting chives is slightly reduced if they're placed near other plants.

The one thing you should know is that chives quickly grow and can easily take over the container where they are growing. You shouldn't allow them to be in the same container as others. They need their own space where they are happy.

Chives are extremely easy to grow since they are difficult to kill. Chives can be difficult to kill even for the most diligent gardener. They make a great plant to start with.

Cilantro

Cilantro is another commonly grown herb. However, it can be more challenging to grow than other herbs. Cilantro is delicious when fresh and can be used to spice up any dish. Remember that cilantro can't be transplanted well. It will remain in the same place you planted it.

Cilantro can only survive on four hours of direct sunlight per day. It needs periods of shade and reduced light afterward. This makes it a little easier than other plants. It needs sunlight for only a few hours each day. Too much sun can damage the plant by turning it brown and causing it to turn brown.

Cilantro's growth requires that you pay attention to how much water is being used. Like many plants, it is important to inspect the soil and provide water if it becomes dry. As cilantro is very nutrient poor, it needs to be watered frequently. It is important to water cilantro properly. Water should start to seep from drainage holes.

The aggressive nutrient requirements of cilantro make it a complicated plant. Fresh cilantro is delicious!

Basil

Basil is most commonly grown outdoors. However, it can also grow indoors. Basil is a highly aromatic herb that can both be useful in the kitchen or add a pleasant aroma to the home.

Basil needs around six hours of sunlight a day. To get artificial fluorescent light, you will need to use approximately 10. It is possible to use different levels of each without growing problems.

Basil doesn't have a high tolerance for water stress. Soil should be well-drained, but not too soggy. Soggy soil can cause roots to become rotted and the plant will die. Basil will not survive as long as chives.

Basil is also known to grow fast and aggressively. It's best to keep basil in its pot to prevent it leaching nutrients from its neighbor. If you are not able to place the container in sufficient size, you may need to repot the plant for continued growth. Basil transplants well so this need not be a concern.

Basil is middle of a difficult list. It can be difficult for basil to water properly, but because it is so fast growing, you can be quite lax sometimes.

Mint

Mint is a common and easy to grow herb. It is ideal for an indoor garden. Mint can also be grown in small spaces. Therefore, a small windowill or balcony is sufficient space for this herb. Mint can also be easily cared for by gardeners.

Mint only needs 4 hours of sun per day. It can also enjoy some shade. This plant does well in morning sun with afternoon shade. Direct sunlight can cause the plant to burn. It is best to place it about a foot away from a window that receives indirect light.

To water, water only when the soil feels dry to your touch. Mint is able to withstand drought, so you don't have to water it often. You are more likely to water your underwater mint than you will overwater it.

Mint is like chives in that it can quickly grow and take over its own container. To avoid any problems with plants nearby, mint should be kept in its own pot. Although this can be a problem, it does allow you to grow quite a bit of mint in surprisingly short time.

Fruits

A great alternative for indoor gardening, fruits can be grown indoors but many gardeners hesitate to try them. Although fruits are more difficult to grow that herbs, they are definitely doable and well-worth the effort. Homegrown fruits have a delicious taste. The sensation of biting into freshly picked fruit is truly unique.

You should remember that most fruits are light intensive. A lot of light is necessary to produce large, beautiful fruits. It is crucial to have the proper lighting for fruits that come from tropical locations.

Strawberries

Although strawberries might not seem like something you would think is easy to grow indoors for, it's far easier than most people realize. Growing strawberries indoors has the added benefit of fewer pests.

Space is the most important consideration for strawberries. Strawberries require lots of room in order to thrive. Hanging baskets, or vertical shelving, are great ways of packing a lot of plants into small spaces. Strawberries might not work well if there isn't enough room to grow them.

Strawberries must have at least six hours of direct sun each day. If the sun is less than 6 hours per day, the plants will not work as well and produce less fruit. The risk is that they will stop producing fruit.

Each day, test strawberries for water. Make sure they get water when the soil is dry. Strawberries have a very shallow root system. It is essential that you water your strawberries regularly. Their roots will not absorb water from deeper soils.

Although strawberries can be tricky to grow, once you are comfortable with the process they will grow easily. It is essential that the roots have enough room to spread. You should provide enough space for them to spread, otherwise they won't grow well.

Tomatoes

Tomatoes grow best outdoors but can also be grown indoors. To produce tomatoes year round, they need to be grown indoors as they do not bear fruit in winter. Take into account that although tomatoes grown indoors are healthy, they tend to be smaller than their outdoor counterparts.

Tomatoes should have full sunlight for at most 8 hours per day. This is vital for tomato production and should not be overlooked. It is common for people to have trouble growing tomatoes outdoors. If you are planning on growing the plant indoors, you may want to consider purchasing grow lights.

Temperature is another crucial factor in tomato development. Keep the tomato plants in an area of 65 degrees Fahrenheit. It is important to keep the tomatoes away from any cold blasts or drafts.

Keep the soil well-watered for best results. Water your plants when the soil starts drying out. Tomatoes have a fickle growth process. If the soil is left too dry, it can lead to disaster.

While tomatoes are not easy to grow at the beginning, they can be very difficult to grow. If you don't have enough light, your tomatoes won't produce any edible fruit. You can achieve this level of light, and then it's pretty simple.

Lemon Trees

A lemon tree, or any other citrus fruit tree, is a good option for those who want something a bit bigger. These trees require some attention and are not an easy task. But the reward is well-worth it. Although they may seem difficult, you can learn how to care for indoor lemon trees.

As you might imagine, a lemon trees will need plenty of light. The ideal time for a lemon tree is 8+ hours of sunshine per day. Without sunlight, a weak tree will not bear any harvestable fruit.

A fair amount of water is necessary for lemon trees. Follow the same advice as above and water lemon trees once they reach touch 1-2". Be prepared to do this more often than other plants. Lemon trees can be thirsty and will dry out faster than most other plants. It is important to make sure your soil is being checked daily in order to keep your plant hydrated.

Lemon trees require regular feeding, which is usually once per month during the summer/spring. This provides enough nutrients to help them grow and maintain their size.

As a final piece of advice, try to find dwarf varieties for indoor growing. These are specifically designed to be smaller than traditional tree varieties. They can still reach heights exceeding 10' so the term "small" is not accurate.

But, it's still way smaller than a traditional lime tree.

Vegetables

A great addition to any meal is vegetables. Access to fresh, readily available vegetables is great for anyone who wants to be healthier. Being able to access fresh vegetables all year makes this easier. However, nothing beats the freshness you get from growing your own veggies. Much like fruits, veggies can be quite labor intensive and require careful attention in order to produce delicious ingredients. However, there are many low-macitence vegetable options that you can begin your gardening journey.

Scallions

Scallions are great indoor vegetable choices. Similar to chives' strong smell, scallions can provide natural pest control to your garden. Scallions, just like chives and chives, are easy to grow, so even novices can easily take them on.

Scallions require approximately 6 hours sunlight per day. Rotating the container every 2-3 days is a great tip to ensure that every plant receives equal sunlight. Scallions prefer moist, but not soaked soil. You can provide some water prior to and right after the sprouting of seeds. However, they will slow down in growth as they age.

Overall, scallions grow easily. They are also very hardy, and like chives, they are difficult to kill. They have very standard needs and can be used for most gardening advice.

Eggplants

Although the eggplants are smaller when grown indoors they are still delicious. Indoors, you have complete control of the environment. This is especially helpful for eggplant lovers who are sensitive to temperature.

Despite that, this is probably the most difficult item to grow.

Important to consider is their space requirements. Eggplants are large. They need to be grown in a large, well-lit container. Like strawberries, this plant is not for those who are limited on space.

It is also because eggplants are slow growers. Do not get discouraged if it takes months for you to find the right specimen. It doesn't matter what you do, eggplants just take a long time to mature.

Bright sunlight should be available for at least 12-14 hour a day. These are the most basic needs of most people.

Water is also a concern. An issue with eggplants is the root drying out and not getting enough moisture. Don't hesitate to add a little water before the soil dries completely.

Eggplants will not be for the faint of heart. They can be very challenging to grow, as they have high requirements in all categories. It might not be the best option for beginners, but those looking to grow are sure to find it rewarding.

Lettuce

Lettuce along with many other leafy vegetables are very well-loved garden items because of their versatility and ease in growing. Lettuce can also be grown indoors with very little care.

Start by giving your lettuce at least 6+ hours of indirect sunlight per day. Direct sunlight is best avoided as it can both burn out leaves and also cause bolting. Bolting is the process of a plant becoming bloated. It occurs when it begins to flower. This makes the plant unpalatable. Bolting can be caused a lot by heat so keep your lettuce in a cool location to extend its harvest lifespan.

Lettuce is drought-tolerant, so it doesn't need much water. Every few days, check it and if the top 2-3 inches of soil are dry, give it a healthy dose. Lettuce can be left alone and will not require frequent watering. If it's in a cooler environment, the soil will stay moister for longer.

Lettuce can be grown indoors in a very simple way. They grow quickly, can be cared for easily, and require little maintenance.

Flowers (non edible)

An indoor plant collection is incomplete without a section on flowers. A basket of flowers is a great way to add beauty and elegance to your home. Although not as tasty as other types, they are more pleasing to the eye and less difficult to grow.

Peace Lily

Because of their ease of cultivation, peace Lilies are popular among beginner gardeners. This flower is commonly found in offices as well as homes. It can add beauty and color to any room and is low maintenance.

The Peace lily can withstand low to moderate lighting. This makes it a great choice for rooms in your home where there isn't enough light for other more difficult plants. The whiter the flower blooms, however, the less light it receives.

You should water them at least once per week. You should water them when the soil is dry. Peace lilies tolerate less water than peace lilies so don't overwater them.

You should choose peace lilies as a starting plant if it is easy to care for. They are both very easy to keep alive and to maintain, making them a good first choice. They also have low maintenance requirements.

Ficus

Another very popular indoor flower is the Ficus. They are almost miniature trees that have a single trunk and a wide canopy of leaves. Despite their popularity they can be a little tricky to manage.

Even at a large size, the ficus can still maintain its original shape. Place your ficus in a container that will accommodate the desired size.

A bright, indirect, and even direct light is ideal for light. The leaves can be burned if placed in direct sunlight. They don't like cold. Keep them at least 60 degrees and ideally 70+.

You must keep your plant's moisture levels high. You can mist the leaves lightly to keep them moist. They will not tolerate being soaked in water. Do not water the soil if it is still damp.

Common Mistakes & FAQ

I wanted to include a section on common questions that indoor gardeners often have. These are some of the common questions I receive and have tried to gather them all in one place. This chapter is designed to help you quickly get answers to your questions and problems.

What plants are the best for indoors?
Most plants can be grown indoors if you provide the right conditions. However the best indoor plants are those that can grow in low light conditions. These include plants such:

Peace Lily
Snake Plant
Mint
Chives

Among many more. While this doesn't mean other plants can't be done, it does mean that they are more difficult to maintain.
What soil should I use when growing an indoor garden in my backyard?
Use soil that is marked as potting soil, and specifically designed for containers. Normal top soil can be too compacted

and may not drain well if placed in containers. It is easy to tell the differences by simply picking up a bag. Potting soil feels lighter and airier.

There are many types and brands of potting soil. Citrus blends may be more suitable for some plant types but aren't essential. Only soil for succulents or cacti is an exception. This soil is often coarser than standard soil, and it encourages faster draining. These types of plants will not survive in normal potting dirt.

Should I Change the Soil in My Home?

You should change the soil around every two years. This is due to the fact that soil tends towards compacting over time. This decreases drainage, and can hinder a plants ability absorb nutrients. This is when your plants are most likely to be ready for growth and at their best.

What is Overwatering and how can it be used?

Overwatering is when you give too much water. This will cause the plant to become irritated and eventually, it will end up in the soil. Water stored in a container does not have any place to go. So it will remain in the soil. This can cause root rot which is a bacterial disease that can kill your plant. If you water your plants correctly and have good drainage, you can avoid root rot and other related problems.

What are the Signs of Water Overwatering

As many of these signs are similar to each other, it can be hard for you to determine if something is wrong. However, falling or growing leaves are a sure sign that there are problems. The soil should be checked for moisture. This could indicate root rot.

It is essential to inspect roots to ensure 100% accuracy. Roots affected with root rot are likely to look brownish and feel mushy. The soil might also smell rotten.

Why are my Leaves turning yellow

It can be caused by a variety issues but it is most commonly related to the sun and watering. It's important to take care of your plants and fix any problems. It will take some time and trial and error to determine the cause.

How often should I water my indoor plants

This will vary depending on the plant. However, there are some general rules. Most indoor plants require watering about once every 1-2 week. The best way to prevent overwatering is to touch the soil at the surface.

Certain plants require water differently. Cacti may go without water for many weeks, while tomatoes that are actively growing require it only every few days.

Other environmental factors include temperature, humidity and airflow.

Can a plant get too much sun?

Yes, too high sun can cause leaf browning. Plants do not always need full sun. However, too much sun can be harmful to low-light plants.

It is important to also consider sun intensity. Some plants need indirect light. Indirect light is like moving the plant back from a sunny windowsill. These plants can be affected by too much sunlight. Be sure to provide your plants with the right amount and intensity of light.

Why are my plants bent?

This is often because the majority of the sun they receive comes from one direction. Plants are inclined to grow towards the sun, so if there is only one direct, they will be more inclined to grow in that direction.

Rotating your plants once per week is an easy way to fix this problem. This allows them to have even lighting and prevents imbalances.

This is related to a plant that grows tall but is not growing fuller. This can be caused by the plant growing to gain more light. Increase the time that the plant is in direct sunlight and stake it to prevent it from falling.

Winter Gardening

A great thing about owning an indoor garden, is the ability to grow it all year. Even in the coldest winters an indoor garden can thrive and produce edible crops or flowers.

Even if you keep your plants indoors there are still dangers. Winter brings new challenges to your plants that can throw you off guard. It is relatively easy to winterproof your indoor gardens. It requires a little thought and planning.

This chapter focuses on exactly that. It will teach you how to prevent the most common problems that winter brings on your garden. The end will provide you with the knowledge to ensure that your garden survives winter's harshest conditions.

It's All Relative

Before we get started, it is important to remember that these issues are very specific to the area you live in. This chapter was written with the Midwest winter in mind. However, it can also be used for cooler areas.

These issues will be less severe in areas that don't see much winter. Some of the advice in this article can be ignored if it is warm year-round. Some of the advice may still apply to your situation, so it's worth taking a look.

There is less sunlight

The sun's intensity is lower during the winter months. This can create problems for gardeners since it means your plants get less sunlight than during the warmer seasons. This may be a problem for your plants.

This is how to make sure your plants have more sun during winter. You could either move them to a better location or use grow lights. Pay attention to signs of sun damage such as reaching, leggy or reaching.

Plant Dormancy

Depending on which plant you have, the winter can cause it to go dormant. This means that it will slow down its development and most likely not produce any edible material. This is normal and what nature does.

You should remember that this slower growth will mean less nutrients and more water. You'll need to fertilize the plant less often or none at all during this time. Reduce the amount you water. This is because your plant isn't actively growing or producing flower, meaning it consumes less energy.

Dry Air

Winter typically brings lower humidity and generally drier temperatures. This is due to the fact that colder air tends to retain less moisture then warm air. For homes using a forced-air furnace, the combustion that heats it removes water vapour from the air. This further reduces humidity. This means that winter humidity will be lower in cold climates than in summer.

This can be dangerous depending on your plants. Humidity levels need to be high for certain plants, especially tropicals. If they fall too low, it can damage the plant. It can also lead to overwatering because gardeners mistakenly think that low humidity is lack of water.

Once you determine that humidity has been a problem, you can take steps in order to increase the humidity. We've discussed several of these techniques, but one of our favorite is to mist the plant every day. If you notice your leaves are falling apart but you continue to water them, this is probably due to the humidity problem that winter brings.

Temperature Changes

The last thing is that winter brings about a lot of temperature changes from indoors to outside, which can have a negative impact on your garden. These are generally the two most dangerous places to plants. They also have the largest temperature swings.

First, you have drafty or poorly-insulated windows and doors. These areas can become a lot more cold than the surrounding environment, which can cause your plant to suffer. Sometimes you may notice that your plant will appear worse if it is facing the source. You must be careful not to place plants in areas where cool air is coming from.

Another issue is proximity to heating equipment such as furnace vents or space heaters. The heat from these vents can be very drying and harmful for plants. To prevent any problems, keep your plants at least a foot away from heat sources.

Greenhouse Gardening

We haven't even touched on greenhouses. Greenhouses offer a safe space for plants and can help extend your growing seasons. If done properly, you may be able enjoy a healthy and vibrant garden all year.

A greenhouse has the great benefit of increasing your indoor space. You have the option to either build a small indoor greenhouse or place it outside. Larger greenhouses can be constructed freestanding or placed against the exterior walls of your house, just like a small garden box.

This section will provide all the information you need to start and grow a greenhouse. We'll first look at the benefits and reasons to open a greenhouse. We will then discuss common greenhouses, and how to set them up. We will then discuss some of the essential considerations and important facts that you need to know about how to run your greenhouse.

Greenhouses: The benefits

Before we dive into the details of how to set up your greenhouse, let's briefly talk about why you might be interested in it. There are many benefits to greenhouses for gardeners. It may also be a good option depending on your gardening goals.

Protects

A greenhouse provides protection and a solid structure for your plants. This shields your plants from the elements that can damage them. This is especially important for seedlings and young plants that can be affected by heavy rain or high winds.

It also offers some protection against pests. Although it's not perfect it can significantly reduce the possibility of bugs infesting your plants. The greenhouse makes it much more difficult for bugs to reach your plants than if they were directly exposed. However, this doesn't eliminate the risk completely. It is still important to inspect your plants for signs of infestation.

It will almost always provide protection against larger animals, like squirrels or deer. These critters are often a problem for gardeners, and can endanger a harvest. If your greenhouse is properly secured, you can avoid these types of animals harming plants. A greenhouse could be the right solution for protecting your plants if your plants are regularly visited by larger animals.

Get More Seasons

A greenhouse can significantly extend your growing season, even with minimal effort. A greenhouse will allow you to plant earlier than normal and can even help you start your garden sooner. This is a major advantage for growers. It allows you to harvest more early and harvest later.

You can take this one step further with some effort. A greenhouse provides a solid base and can be improved to extend your growing season. We'll get to them all in the next section.

Allows Winter Gardening

A greenhouse can allow winter gardening depending on your climate. It is easier to do winter gardening if you have mild winters.

Even those living in colder climates may be able to garden some or all of the winter. Although it can take some time to maintain heat, it is easy once you get the hang of it. If you follow the steps below, you can plant a garden in your greenhouse for all of winter.

Easier Environment Control

Another advantage of greenhouses over outdoor plants is the finer control they offer over the environment. While it may not be as easy to grow plants indoors as in a greenhouse, you can better control the environment, such as temperature, humidity, water, and so on.

There are many methods to adjust these values. The greenhouse temperature can be adjusted to avoid it getting too hot during the summer by a skilled gardener. We'll be discussing how they might do this later in the article.

Faster Plant Growth

In many cases, your plants will grow faster in a greenhouse. This is because greenhouses are designed specifically for plant growth. This makes it a great way to plant seeds or seedlings. It also provides a favorable environment for their growth.

Can You Grow Non-native and Exotic Plants?

Because greenhouses have greater control over the climate, they allow you to choose from a wide range of plant options. Many greenhouses can be used to grow non-native, exotic species. Many gardeners can grow tropical plants indoors in their greenhouses, even in regions that are not favorable to them like the midwest.

How do Greenhouses Function?

It's important to understand how greenhouses work. This will aid us later in choosing the right location for our greenhouse.

Generally, greenhouses are designed to capture the sun's energy and provide warmth for plants. To maximize sunlight, greenhouses can be designed so that plants get as much sun as possible.

For this reason, greenhouses are made mostly of glass and plastic. These materials allow for a lot more sunlight and are the main components of greenhouse construction. Most greenhouses require minimal framing to maximise light intake.

It can also be dangerous. Because greenhouses absorb as much light and are therefore warmer than the natural environment, they are usually more comfortable than the outdoors. This is great in winter and on cool nights, but can cause problems during the heat of summer. When you are planning your greenhouse, remember this.

A Starter Greenhouse

There are many different ways to start your greenhouse. Although greenhouses are often viewed as immovable structures that cannot be moved, it isn't true. There are many sizes and styles of greenhouses available on the marketplace.

Here are some examples for pre-built options in greenhouse construction:

A Small Frame Greenhouse can fit on a porch or in a sunny place in your yard. It's perfect for smaller crops and doesn't take up too much space. These boxes are very similar to a greenhouse, and offer many of same benefits as full greenhouses.

Mini Tiered greenhouse: This tiny treehouse cleverly takes advantage of vertical space. This greenhouse is ideal for those with very little space and is great for anyone looking to start. These are often a type or shelving that has been covered in plastic to provide the benefits and protection of a greenhouse.

Walk-in greenhouse: This is an upgraded version of the traditional greenhouse and allows for easy access. This is for those who require more space and wish to grow larger plants. It is likely to remain in place for longer periods and be harder to move than smaller greenhouses. It is also one of the easiest greenhouses to grow in winter. This gives you more options to conserve heat.

Also, you always have the option of building your own. If you're looking for a green house plan, there are plenty of options. And, of course, you have the freedom to create your own. Many people have used recycled glass and plastic sheets to make their own greenhouses. These can be both functional and fashionable, and they are very affordable.

You should remember that smaller greenhouses may have difficulty keeping heat inside during winter. Many heat improvement techniques will require more space to function properly. It shouldn't stop you from building small greenhouses if it suits your needs. But, consider how you'll heat them in the winter if a year-round garden is what you desire.

These are the Key Considerations

Hopefully, you are now starting to have ideas about how to create the perfect greenhouse. A few important things to remember before you dive into planning. This section will provide information to help you make informed decisions regarding your greenhouse project.

Position and Size

First, you need to know where your greenhouse is located and how big it is.

Your greenhouse's size will usually be dictated by its location. To maximize its potential, make sure your greenhouse is in direct sunlight.

The best news is that there are sizes for just about any location you can imagine. Even a small space on a deck can be enough to make a small greenhouse.

Although it is better to have your greenhouse in bright sunlight, you should be careful how much light it receives. This is especially true for areas that have very hot summers. When you consider how hot your summers get, the greenhouse you have will probably be a few degrees higher.

Depending on your plants, it might even be too warm. There are many methods to reduce heat. However, the easiest way is to put your greenhouse in some shade. If your greenhouse is not capable of sustaining the temperatures, it might be worth getting some shade in the afternoon. Keep in mind that the effects of shade can be carried over to the winter and could cause problems as temperatures drop.

Also, consider the possibility of extreme weather when planning your greenhouse location. There are many horror stories about powerful storms that can destroy greenhouses.

The best foundation and protection for the greenhouse is important, but you can also position it to minimize the storm's effect. The greenhouse can be placed in an area that receives partial coverage, such close to your home or garage, to limit the storm's effect. This is important to remember if you live close to an area with extreme weather. As we will see, these lean to greenhouses can offer additional benefits beyond protection from the elements.

Foundation and stability

You'll need to plan how you're going provide enough stability for the greenhouse to withstand strong storms, especially if it's larger. Inadequately secured greenhouses can easily be destroyed by wind or storms.

Most kits and plans come with attachments or holes that will help secure your garden. These may be screws you need to drill into a foundation.

It is a good idea, if you are looking for a foundation for your greenhouse, to build one that is simple. It not only gives the greenhouse stability, but also seals it against pests and rodents. Gardeners tend to use concrete or wood for their foundations. It's important that you start with a flat ground or work your way up.

Indoor Decorations

It's not a must, but you need to think about how your greenhouse interior will look. Many people will have shelves in their garden, while others will prefer containers and planters.

You are not restricted in this area. It really depends upon the types of plants that are being grown.

This allows you to have complete creative control over the design and construction of your greenhouse. Even a tiny greenhouse is a chance to put your stamp on it. There are so many great greenhouse design ideas, so get creative.

Heat

Growing greenhouses can be difficult due to heat. It is okay to have heat, but not too much can cause plants to suffer. A key part of successful greenhouse management involves controlling heat. This will be broken down in two sections. The first is to increase the heat. Both are required and have their respective tricks.

In either case the goal of any greenhouse is to keep the temperature relatively constant throughout the day. You should avoid big swings and make changes gradually, as it is in nature. A good thermometer will be essential if you want to grow in a greenhouse.

Reduce heat

A lot of greenhouses will need to be cooled in summer. It is better to be proactive than reactive and do something before the temperature goes too high. This helps to avoid overexposing your plants to heat. But it's often easier to do this before it gets too warm.

Here are some ways you can reduce the heat inside your greenhouse.

Be mindful of your location

The climate of your greenhouse can play a significant role in its heat. The greenhouse heats up faster if there is more sun. It can also be less hot if the greenhouse is located in shade.

The point of a greenhouse is to get plenty sun, so don't be too shady.

Consider a location that is shaded in the afternoon, if heat is an issue. This provides a balance of bright, sunny days with the possibility to cool off in the evening.

Your greenhouse should be kept in the shade when it is more temperate. You won't likely need any shade, depending on how hot you are in summer. These tips will help you to mitigate heat, so even if your home is in full sunlight, you have options.

Open Roof Vents

Roof vents are a common feature in large greenhouses. Hot air rises. Roof vents will help move heat out of your greenhouse.

Some larger greenhouses may also have side vents or opening windows. They all provide heat escape routes and serve the same purpose.

Open the Door

Similar to vents you can prop open the doors of your greenhouse to release heat. You can also pair this with fan-powered vents to quickly reduce heat.

Use a fan

Good ventilation is vital. We'll be discussing it more later. It can help reduce heat. A fan will speed up the cycle of air, so be sure to pair it in conjunction with an open or vented door.

Water the Ground

Another option is watering the ground in your greenhouse. This is called damping. This happens because as water evaporates off the ground, it raises the humidity in your greenhouse and decreases the temperature.

It's smart to do this frequently, as the additional humidity is good for plants. Humidity can be a great help in protecting your plants from heat stress. It can also prevent some bugs from getting into your plants, so it is a win in several ways.

Shade Cloths

Shade cloths can be special-made fabrics that block the sun's UV light. You can get as much as 50% to 30% blocking, while others block at least 30%. These are great options, but will block any light that is not needed.

Don't Go Overboard

Although it is important to reduce heat, it is also important not too much. As you will see, greenhouses can have difficulty keeping heat up once the sun goes down. This means you must ensure your greenhouse keeps enough heat to keep it warm throughout the night. Reduced heat can lead to damage to plants after the sun goes down.

The rising heat

On the other hand, sometimes you want your greenhouse to be warmer. This is typically the case in winter when temperatures drop drastically. Although greenhouses do a good job at absorbing heat but they also lose heat quickly because of poor insulation.

This can make it difficult to heat your greenhouse in the colder months. There are many options available to increase your greenhouse's heat.

Position is the first thing to do.

Your position can play a significant role in increasing heat. Your greenhouse will receive more warmth the sunnier it is.

It is possible to also place your greenhouse in an area that will help it heat up or insulate. This is a typical greenhouse design. This setup places the greenhouse on the wall opposite the garage or house.

This wall not only has insulation properties, but it can also radiate heat depending what is on the other side. This can make your greenhouse more efficient by providing an active heat source. Consider a lean-to layout if your goal is to grow winter vegetables.

Thermal Mass

Another tip: Add items with a higher thermal Mass to your greenhouse. The ability of a material to absorb or radiate heat is known as thermal mass. The most common greenhouse building materials, such as plastic and glass have a low thermal Mass. They are able to absorb heat but lose it quickly.

It's important to use items that have high thermal mass. Water is the easiest item to use. You can use large containers of water to provide your greenhouse with lots of high-temperature mass material, which is very affordable.

Place the water containers in large containers. The sunlight will heat water during the day. The heat of the sun will heat water, then the temperature of your greenhouse will rise at night. The larger the effect, water will be used more.

A few other lesser-used alternatives include:

* Dense concrete block
* Bricks
* Stones

Use a Heater

If all else fails a heater is always an option. The heater is usually temporary and can be combined using thermal mass to keep the heat going for longer.

Place the heater away from your plants. The heat could damage them. Make sure to observe safety precautions. The heater should be checked frequently. The last thing that you want is for your greenhouse to catch fire.

Air Circulation

A second important consideration is air circulation in your garden. Proper airflow has many benefits for your plants.

* Promotes healthy plant growth
* Helps regulate temperature
* Helps prevent certain pests

Lots of gardeners face problems when starting their greenhouses because they have poor airflow.

It is quite simple to achieve proper air flow. A gentle breeze through your garden is often enough.

This can usually be accomplished by opening the roof vents up and propping open the doors. These two will create a nice cross breeze, and help bring fresh air into your greenhouse. If you want to make the airflow even more efficient, you can install a small fan.

Flooring & Drainage

If your greenhouse is large enough, you'll probably need to plan for flooring. The most plans and building materials only provide the frame, leaving the floor to you.

A greenhouse floor has two main functions. It will drain excess water and stop weed growth. There are many options. We'll only recommend the one that is most popular with greenhouse growers.

First, cover the area in which your greenhouse will go up with weed tarp. This will create a thick barrier that will stop weeds growing in your greenhouse. This step should not be neglected as it is easier to prevent them from appearing than to deal successfully with them once the have started to appear.

Many people use stones and small pebbles for the flooring. This provides a solid surface that can withstand dirt and water. Greenhouses can sometimes get messy so it is crucial to have a floor which is easy to spill on. This will also allow you to water and "dampen down" the floor, as discussed above.

Popular Greenhouse Uses

Now we have covered the most important aspects of setting up a greenhouse and how to run it. I want to discuss some of the specific reasons that people construct a greenhouse.

Each section gives tips and tricks for using your greenhouse for specific purposes. There are many ways to use your greenhouse. Don't think you have to just choose one.

Starting Seeds in A Greenhouse

Many people use their greenhouse as a perfect place to start seeds. Because of the high temperature/high humidity, greenhouses can be very helpful in seed growth. This makes the greenhouse the perfect place for planting seeds and seedlings.

Most gardeners will use seed trays to start seeds and grow a large number of plants at once. This will give you a better chance to have a successful plant, since it's rare that all seeds sprout.

Beyond that, your primary concern will be temperature. You don't want it to drop below freezing. This is often true for gardeners who start their seeds when temperatures are still low at night. You must ensure that the temperature doesn't drop too low. Many seeds won't germinate if the soil isn't warm enough. You can then follow standard seeding instructions.

You can start the season early or you can go late

Many gardeners also make use of their greenhouses to start in the spring and finish in autumn earlier than natural times. This allows them more harvest in a single growing season.

This is a good option for those who live in harsh winter areas and don't want to keep their greenhouse warm all winter. It is often easy enough for spring/fall to do this, and the longer growing season makes it well worth the effort, even if there isn't much use in winter.

Many gardeners also plan to move plants out of the greenhouse as soon as summer begins. Depending on your timing this could help reduce high heat or eliminate them entirely. If there are no plants within the greenhouse, it won't affect how much heat is generated.

Be aware that outdoor plants can have the same difficulties as indoor plants moving from a garden to an outside environment. Be sure to give your plants adequate time to adjust.

Growing through Winter

The greenhouse is probably the most well-known image. It's a place where your plants can grow in comfort, surrounded by snowy winter landscape. While winter gardening can be done, it is not always easy if the winter is harsh.

Heat is the key issue. It can be difficult for plants to retain heat during winter. While some plants may go dormant for the winter and can live at lower temperatures than others, winters with hard frosts are going to be too harsh on most plants.

The easiest option is to add some thermal mass in your greenhouse, depending on how low it gets. While this can help, it will not be enough in order to combat extremely cold temperatures. This is why you might want to pair it with a heater. This is especially true at night when it is difficult to get any sun-generated warmth.

Lack of sunlight during winter could also be an issue, as mentioned above. This is especially true when you have tropical or exotic plants that require full sunlight all year. If you have these plants, you will need to make a grow lighting setup. Depending on what type of lights you have, this may provide some additional heat. Make sure to not burn your plants.

One tip for winter growers: Plants that are naturally more resilient against frost and cold is a good idea. Some leafy greens, such as Kale, can be grown in colder temperatures than other plants. Starting with plants that can grow in cooler conditions reduces the effort it takes to keep your greenhouse hot.

Remember to take into account the material used in building your greenhouse. All plastics are not created equal and some plastics retain heat better than others. In general, the more expensive materials will make it harder for them to maintain an even temperature in winter. If you live somewhere with very cold winters, you may want to invest in high-quality gardening materials.

Greenhouse Additions

Even though this is all the essentials, many people also add their own features to their greenhouse. These are usually used to fix a problem like excessive heat or help them manage their plants better.

This step is completely optional. It's up to the individual gardener what they want. We won't go into too much detail, each of these could take over its own chapter. Some of the most requested additions are:

* Setting up timers or grow lights
* Remote control of automatic vents
* Adding lights at night for better visibility
* Built-in fans and heating
* Self-watering and irrigation system

There are endless possibilities, and your imagination truly is the only limit. To improve your greenhouse, think about the problems that you are facing and then find ways to solve them.

Greenhouses Review

Now we are done with the introduction to greenhouses. Although there are many things we could say, these should provide you with a good foundation to continue your research.

Granges can help you extend your growing seasons and provide your plants with a safe haven. A well-placed greenhouse will dramatically increase your harvest yields. With a little bit of care, you can grow plants all year, even in the dead season.

9 Steps for Your Own Garden

Now that you have read all about the basics of starting a gardening business, it's now time to get out there. The previous pages have a lot to offer, so I've made the following steps to help you get started.

Each step is an actionable thing you can do right away. Once you're done with them, your garden is ready for you to enjoy!

1. Find a place to grow: Take a good look around your house. Be sure to look for spaces near windows that get lots of sunlight. However, you must not forget about other areas that are suitable for

low-light plants. Calculate how much space it takes to start. If you're starting out, start small. It's possible to expand your garden in the future. Hanging or tiered gardens may be a better option if you are short on space. These gardens can make more of your space by using vertical space.

2. Decide on the right plant: Once your location is chosen and you have an idea of the lighting, it's time to determine what type you want to plant. The first step is to identify the type of plant (veggie and fruit, herb and flower), then narrow down your search. Next, you will need to determine which plants belong in the category that best suits your lighting situation. Finally, you need to ensure that the chosen plant can be grown in the available space. A sunny windowsill may be great for chives, but is not ideal for an eggplant. Grow lights can also be used. A grow light is a great

idea if you have a good area with low light levels.

3. Read on: Once you have your plant selected, take a moment to read about it. It is important to look at how to care for your plant, what you can do with it, and what the soil choice should be. This will give solid information that you can use for the next few steps. All the tips in this book are important, but you should also add the specifics about your plant.

4. Make a decision about the container: Once you have done some research you should have an idea of the type of container you should choose. Material isn't a big deal. It's only the size that really matters. You should ensure you select a container large enough to hold the plant and also allow for growth. It is important to consider the dimensions of the container in order to accommodate the root structure. Proper drainage is essential too.

5. Get some soil. Every plant needs soil to grow. You have done all the research. Now go to the store and get the potting mix that suits your plant. Most types of commercial pot soil work with most plants. But, succulents and other delicate plants may require different soil.

6. Plant it: Now it's time to start planting! Either purchase seeds or a small seedling. It is usually easier to start from seeds, but can be more costly. Whatever your preference, prepare your soil and seeds in a container. Then place the seeds/seedlings in the appropriate space. It will depend on the size of the plant that you have, so space between them may vary. Most plants like between 8-12", but it may vary depending on your plant.

7. Setting a maintenance routine: Once you have placed your plants in their new home, it is a good idea. It doesn't

take much to give them a quick inspection in the morning. This may seem like a lot, but it can have serious benefits. Even if you only spend 30 seconds checking on your plants each day, this is still a significant time investment. It will not only help ensure that they get enough water, but also allow you to spot any problems or pests before they become bigger issues.

8. Harvest: This is the time when you can reap the benefits of your work, if you are growing an edible/harvestable variety. It depends on what kind of plant you have, but usually within a few moists you will be able and able to use your plant.

It is important to prune and cut back the plant occasionally, even if your goal is to not eat it. This keeps your plant healthy and beautiful.

9. Repeat: Once one plant has been successfully grown, there's no stopping

you pursuing more. Learn all you can and get out there to enjoy the joys of gardening.